VITAL
GUIDE

COMMANDERS AND HEROES OF THE AMERICAN CIVIL WAR

JONATHAN SUTHERLAND

Airlife

Dedication
For Tim Hall

Copyright © 2002 Airlife Publishing Ltd

Text written by Jonathan Sutherland

First published in the UK in 2002
by Airlife Publishing Ltd

British Library Cataloguing-in-Publication Data
A catalogue record for this book
is available from the British Library

ISBN 1 84037 374 1

Typeset by Gray Publishing, Tunbridge Wells, Kent
Printed in Hong Kong

*Contact us for a free catalogue that describes the complete
range of Airlife books.*

Airlife Publishing Ltd
101 Longden Road, Shrewsbury, SY3 9EB, England
E-mail: sales@airlifebooks.com
Website: www.airlifebooks.com

Contents

Introduction

As the North and South divided and prepared for war in 1861, comrades-in-arms who had known one another since their days at West Point went their separate ways. For some of the future commanders of divisions, corps or whole armies, the decision was easy, as they pledged their allegiance to their native states. For others the decision was a more philosophical one and for their families an unpopular one.

Rank and file officers during the Civil War were fifteen per cent more likely to be killed on the battlefield than an enlisted man. Indeed, even a general, who inevitably led from the front, was fifty per cent more likely to become a casualty than a regular soldier.

In making any selection of commanders or heroes of the American Civil War it is inevitable that certain favourites and well-known names are omitted. This book has aimed to provide a mixture of old and young, rich and poor, from the widest backgrounds and motives.

The term 'hero' very much depends on the reader's viewpoint. The inclusion of characters such as Nathan Bedford Forrest or John Singleton Mosby in no way implies their heroism or lack of it. Equally, individuals who proved themselves to many to be utterly incompetent on the battlefield are not included merely for comic relief: they illustrate the fact that good or bad, many officers were elevated to positions during the Civil War to which they could patently not do justice.

Amongst the leading military figures are a number of individuals, including ordinary soldiers, spies and civilians, both African-American and white, who showed their own degrees of valour and self-sacrifice in upholding their beliefs.

The American Civil War raged on land and sea for almost five years. From the very beginning, the Confederacy, although blessed with some of the bolder and more competent commanders, such as Robert E. Lee and 'Stonewall' Jackson, faced the unenviable task of defending over 4,000 miles of frontier against the numerically superior Union army and navy. It was not until the emergence of northern

Civil War Monument in Washington DC. *(John Dunnett)*

commanders, such as Ulysses S. Grant, William T. Sherman and Philip Sheridan, that the full might of the Union army could be wielded with any great precision. Manpower was also a considerable problem for the South; its population was smaller and its political and social system did not allow it to enlist African-American soldiers. This was unlike the North, which from 1863 raised over a hundred regiments of black soldiers, which only served to add additional pressure to the faltering fortunes of the Confederacy.

Although there were over 1,000 battles fought during the American Civil War, the vast majority centred in just four major theatres. In the east, with the opposing capitals within a few days' march of one another, there were continual campaigns which ebbed north and south, bringing about huge battles, such as Gettysburg, Chancellorsville and the two engagements at Bull Run. The control of the Mississippi and the Tennessee rivers created two other major campaign regions. A series of battles culminating in the capture of Vicksburg and Port Hudson left the Mississippi in Union hands. On the Tennessee, after Shiloh, Chattanooga and Chickamauga, the Union troops were able to press deep into Southern-held territory and overrun Georgia and South Carolina. In the far west as far as the Mexican border, both sides pressed Native American Indians into action as vast, thinly held territories were contested.

Civil War armies were complex organisations. Army commanders gave their officers who led corps or divisions a good deal of independence. Army commanders were often full generals but more commonly lieutenant- or major-generals. At corps level the ranks were usually lieutenant- or major-general, whilst major-generals or brigadier-generals commanded divisions. Within each division were a number of brigades, which could be commanded by either brigadier-generals or colonels. Lower down the rankings colonels or majors would lead a regiment.

Wherever possible the individuals featured in this book have been researched to cover their lives and exploits both before and after the American Civil War. For some career officers the Civil War offered them an opportunity to accelerate their promotion and as a result helped to establish them as military professionals.

For all too many, however, the war ruined the individuals featured in the book, along with numerous untold others, physically, mentally or financially, and proved to be the most significant period of their lives.

Equestrian monument to 'Stonewall' Jackson at Manassas.
(John Dunnett)

Archer, James Jay (1817–64)

James J. Archer was born in Harford County, Maryland, to a distinguished family, and attended the United States Military Academy at West Point, together with Albert Sidney Johnston and E. Kirby Smith in 1826. When he left the Academy he was attached to the 3rd Infantry and was promoted to first lieutenant in October 1833. He left the army in 1847 and worked as a civilian until 1861.

On 16 March 1861 James Archer was commissioned into the regular army of the Confederate States as a captain, and was swiftly promoted to Colonel of the 5th Texas Regiment. By May of the same year he was acting brigadier-general, and after the death of Hatton at Seven Pines, Archer was given command of his brigade in A.P. Hill's division and promoted to brigadier-general. His brigade was predominantly made up of Tennessee and Alabama regiments.

James Archer was well respected for his leadership, gallantry and valour in the face of the enemy. Under Archer's leadership the Confederates fought hard during the summer of 1862 at Mechanicsville (26 June), they gained distinction at Gaines's Mill (27 June), were in action at Cedar Mountain (9 August) and fought alongside 'Stonewall' Jackson at Manassas Junction (26 August) and in the battles of Manassas (28–30 August). During the Maryland Campaign James Archer was involved in the battles of Harper's Ferry, Sharpsburg and Shepherdstown, and by Christmas 1862 he and his brigade were heavily involved in the Fredericksburg fighting.

By April 1863 Archer, still under Jackson, fought at Chancellorsville and led a division of Henry Heth's corps in the advance of Gettysburg (1–3 July). On the first day of fighting at Gettysburg James Archer was wounded and taken prisoner by the Union's 'Iron Brigade'. He was imprisoned at Johnson's Island, Ohio, but was later exchanged and sent to join the Army of Tennessee on 9 August 1864. He was to spend only ten days with this army before being transferred to the Army of Northern Virginia, where he took command of two consolidated brigades of Heth's division.

James Archer was to spend only a few weeks here before he died, on 24 October 1864, as a result of the effects of his imprisonment and his wounds.

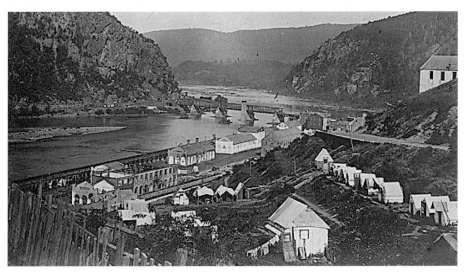

James Archer was involved in the battle of Harper's Ferry. (National Archive)

(Library of Congress)

Lewis Addison Armistead was born to General Walker Keith Armistead and his wife Elizabeth (Stanly) on 18 February 1817 at New Bern, North Carolina. He entered West Point (United States Military Academy) as a cadet in 1834, but resigned or was expelled as a result of an incident involving his classmate Jubal Early. Apparently Armistead, during a disagreement, cracked a mess hall plate over Early's head. He did, however, proceed with a military career, and in 1839 became a second lieutenant in the 6th US Infantry.

March 1844 saw Armistead promoted to first lieutenant, and he entered the war with Mexico, during which he was promoted to the brevet rank of captain for his gallantry, and then brevet major. In 1855 he was formally promoted to the rank of captain.

At the outbreak of the American Civil War Armistead resigned from the United States army and was given the rank of major in the Confederate army on 16 March 1861. Later during the same year Armistead was promoted to colonel and given command of the 57th Virginia Regiment.

By April 1862 Armistead had been promoted to brigadier-general, and had been assigned command of a brigade in the division of Benjamin Huger. Leading this brigade, Armistead was distinguished for personal bravery at Seven Pines and Richmond (25 June). After this campaign he was highly respected as a leader, and was given command of a brigade made up of the 9th, 14th, 38th, 53rd and 57th Virginia Regiments.

At the beginning of the Maryland Campaign (6 September), Armistead was assigned the duty of Provost-Marshal-General of the army, during which time he was involved at Harper's Ferry and Shepherdstown, fighting alongside General George Pickett.

Armistead's most famous service was at the battle of Gettysburg (July 1863). It was here that he was said to have led his men in advance of his brigade, waving his hat in the air, until the Confederate colours were planted over the Union fortifications. It was here, during Pickett's Charge, that Armistead fell mortally wounded and was captured by the Union army. He died two days later on 5 July 1863 at Spangler's Farm.

UNION
Bailey, Joseph (1825–67)

Joseph Bailey was born on 6 May 1825 near Pennsville, Ohio, and he spent his pre-war years working first as a lumberman and then as a civil engineer.

After the commencement of the war in 1861, Bailey joined the 4th Wisconsin in July as a captain, where he served under Generals Banks and Butler in the Department of the Gulf.

By June 1864 Bailey had been promoted to colonel, and was the chief engineer of Franklin's 19th Corps. He was involved in the capture of New Orleans and became the acting chief engineer in charge of the defences of the city. He was also involved and distinguished in the capture of Port Hudson, and remained with General Banks during the Red River Campaign. This joint expedition by the combined army and navy was a failure. Many of the navy's fleet had been left stranded in a dangerously exposed position because of low water levels, and it was Bailey, as chief engineer, who was left to find the solution to the problem. He, along with 3,000 troops, constructed a dam across the river, enabling the vessels to float down on 12 May 1864. Apparently he had been told by Admiral David Dixon Porter that he had twelve days and no money available to him, so he used lumberjacks from the 29th and 23rd Wisconsin and a unit from Maine to build the dam. After sinking two barges and using felled trees and rocks to build the dam, Bailey managed to raise the water level by 7 ft in only eleven

days. For his gallant and innovative efforts Bailey was given a brevet as brigadier and was given the Thanks of Congress – the only one of fourteen given in total to a non-army or corps commander.

By 7 August 1864 Bailey had been promoted to full brigadier-general, and he joined forces with Admiral Farragut in Mobile Harbour, commanding a section of the 13th Army Corps. He was involved in improving the defences at Fort Morgan, constructing a telegraph and building a railroad, repairing wharves and barges and directing the engineers throughout the whole campaign.

Joseph Bailey became a Missouri sheriff after resigning from the army on 7 July 1865. He was shot and killed on 21 March 1867 whilst arresting a group of bushwhackers.

(National Archive) 3

Barton, Clarissa Harlow (Clara) (1821–1912)

Clara Barton was born on Christmas Day, 1821, the youngest of five children of her farmer father, in Oxford, Massachusetts. She was taught at home, and at the age of 15 she embarked on an eighteen-year teaching career. In 1854 she moved to Washington, DC, and by 1861 she was working for the US Patent Office.

In April 1861 the 6th Massachusetts Regiment arrived in Washington, many of them suffering badly from the results of their battles in the Baltimore riots. Clara Barton began the first of her own campaigns to ease the suffering of others by tearing up old sheets for use as bandages and by cooking for the troops – initially those injured in First Bull Run. She also began advertising for provisions in *Spy*, and set up a distribution agency. She applied for permission from the government in 1862 to accompany the sick who were being transported from the battlefields, and was granted a pass to travel in the army ambulances.

Clara travelled in this way throughout Virginia and South Carolina, and worked in hospitals after the battle of Wilderness. She also served as the superintendent of nurses in Major-General Benjamin F. Butler's command.

After the war Clara continued her aid to soldiers by assisting the Union army in locating missing soldiers, whilst also delivering lectures on her experiences. She also became involved in the suffrage movement and became an activist for black rights.

Clara also became active in the International Red Cross, and was awarded the Iron Cross of Merit from the German Emperor in 1873. She saw the need for the American Red Cross, and her efforts were rewarded when John D. Rockefeller funded the opening of its headquarters in Washington in 1881. Clara remained the president for 23 years. At the age of 70 she was involved in transporting supplies to Cuba; at 79 she spent six weeks in Galveston helping those who had been victims of the Texas floods.

Clara resigned her post as president in 1904 and retired to Glen Echo, Maryland. She died at the age of 91, and her body was returned to her native Oxford for burial.

4   *(Library of Congress)*

Powhatan Beaty was born on 8 October 1837 in Richmond, Virginia, but later moved to Ohio as a farmer. He briefly served in the Black Brigade of Cincinnati (2–20 September 1862) when Confederate General Kirby Smith threatened the city. His unit constructed fortifications around Cincinnati before their discharge.

Beaty entered military service on 7 June 1863 at Cincinnati, training at Camp Delaware, and was posted to Company G, 5th United States Colored Infantry (USCT) (127th Ohio Volunteer Infantry). Within two days of his enlistment Beaty was promoted to first sergeant.

In 1864 he marched with Major-General Benjamin Butler's Army of the James to attack the Richmond defences at Fort Harrison, north of the river. Beaty participated in the series of battles of Chaffin's Farm (29–30 September 1864), the assault on New Market Heights being led by Brigadier-General Charles Pain's 3rd Division of the XVIII Corps, USCT. The first assault against General John Gregg's Texas Brigade and the 24th Virginia Cavalry began at 5.30 a.m., and orders were to fix bayonets and to remove the percussion caps of the muskets to prevent accidental firing as the USCT struggled through the Confederate defences. The attack failed, with over fifty per cent casualties, and Powhatan joined the second assault half an hour later.

Major-General Butler was later to report that Beaty took command of Company G

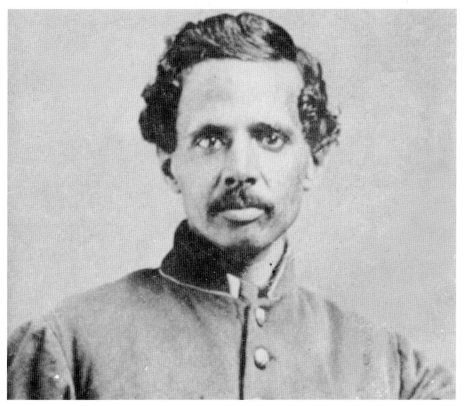

(Library of Congress)

after all of the white officers had been killed or wounded. Beaty and the others involved in this assault were awarded the Medal of Honor for the actions during the day.

... all these gallant colored soldiers were left in command, all their company officers being killed or wounded, and led them gallantly and meritoriously through the day. For these services they have most honorable mention, and the commanding general will cause a special medal to be struck in honor of these gallant colored soldiers.

Beaty was discharged from the army on 6 April 1865. He died on 6 December 1916 and is buried at the Union Baptist Cemetery, Cincinnati, Ohio. A 12 ft portrait of Beaty can be found on Richmond's floodwall, and a bridge on Virginia's Route 5 crossing over the Interstate Route 895 was named the Powhatan Beaty Memorial Bridge.

Beauregard, Pierre Gustave Toutant (1818–93)

(Library of Congress)

Pierre Beauregard was born in Saint Bernard Parish, Louisiana, on 28 May 1818. He attended West Point (United States Military Academy) in 1838, graduating as second in the class and having adopted the nickname of 'The Little Napoleon' because of his admiration of Bonaparte. He was posted to the artillery but transferred only a week later to the engineers. Beauregard became a staff officer with Winfield Scott, and whilst serving in Mexico he was awarded two brevets.

In 1861 Beauregard had been made Superintendent at West Point, but this career proved very short-lived when on 20 February he resigned his commission in the US army and joined the Confederates as a brigadier-general.

Beauregard was placed in charge of the South Carolina troops in Charleston harbour (1 March 1861), where he won the battle at Fort Sumter with very few casualties. From this victory he acquired the nicknames of 'The Hero of Fort Sumter' and 'The Little Creole'.

After Fort Sumter Beauregard was sent to Virginia to command the forces opposite Washington, and here he created the Army of the Potomac, being reinforced by Joseph E. Johnston and his Army of the Shenandoah. This appears to have been the stage at which some conflict between Beauregard and Jefferson Davis began. Apparently at the battle of First Bull Run Beauregard took tactical command whilst Johnston threatened the left flank. Both Beauregard and Johnston complained that their men were inadequately supplied with rations, and that had this not been the case they would have been successful in taking the Union capital. Nevertheless,

Beauregard was promoted to full general status as a result of the battle and was subsequently ordered to join Albert Sidney Johnston as his second-in-command in the western theatre of operations.

Beauregard was responsible for drafting the attack orders for the battle of Shiloh, and he took command of the Army of Tennessee after General Albert Sidney Johnston's death on the battlefield during the first day of fighting. During the evening of the following day Beauregard ordered the calling-off of the attacks, a decision which is still argued over to this day. It is believed by many that his decision allowed the combined armies of Ulysses S. Grant and Don Carlos Buell to drive the Confederates from the battlefield.

After having been forced to evacuate his supply base in Corinth, Mississippi, Beauregard again crossed Jefferson Davis by taking sick leave without permission. As a result he was relieved, by a special order from the President, of his army and its command on 27 June 1862.

By August, however, Beauregard was back in command and held the southern coast from North to South Carolina for over a year and a half. During this time he defended Charleston against naval and ground forces. He was then ordered north and took over command in North Carolina and southern Virginia while Generals Robert E. Lee and Ulysses S. Grant faced one another in northern Virginia.

One of Beauregard's finest victories was his defeat of Benjamin F. Butler at Drewry's Bluff, and from here he began making proposals and plans for an invasion of the North. He also managed to ward off Union attempts to take Petersburg whilst Robert E. Lee was positioned north of the James river, and he remained under the command of Lee during the siege of Petersburg.

In September 1864 Beauregard returned to the western theatre, but this time in overall command of John B. Hood's Army of Tennessee and Richard Taylor's Department of Alabama, Mississippi and East Louisiana. He was unsuccessful in thwarting Sherman during his march to the sea, and by the near-conclusion of the war Beauregard was once more second-in-command to Joseph E. Johnston.

When the war ended, Beauregard returned to New Orleans. He refused a rank in both the Egyptian and Romanian armies, but instead became involved in railroading, and was Louisiana's Adjutant-General. He began a somewhat suspicious and disapproved-of association with the Louisiana Lottery, for which he acted as a supervisor, and also began a short writing career, including one book he co-authored, entitled *A Commentary on the Campaign and Battle of Manassas*.

Pierre Beauregard died on 20 February 1893, and he is buried in Metairie, Louisiana.

Berdan, Hiram (1823–93)

Hiram Berdan was born in Phelps in Ontario County, New York, on 6 September 1823. He was educated as a mechanical engineer and became famous for his inventions, including a repeating rifle, a torpedo boat for evading torpedo nets, a long-distance rangefinder and a distance fuse for shrapnel. Prior to the outbreak of the war Berdan had been the top rifle shot in America for fifteen years and had patented a musket ball.

On 30 November 1861 Berdan was appointed Colonel of the 1st United States Sharpshooters, and was involved in recruiting eighteen companies from eight different states, forming the men into two regiments. He was also in command of sections of the Army of the Potomac

One of Berdan's sharpshooters. (Library of Congress)

during the following two years, having been breveted brigadier-general after Chancellorsville and major-general after Gettysburg, at each of which he led a brigade. He also fought at the Seven Days and Second Bull Run.

The men under Berdan's command had to pass rigorous marksmanship tests and were assigned for special assignments, frequently being used for skirmish duty. Berdan's 1st and 2nd US Sharpshooters were an elite force who wore distinctive green uniforms and were equipped with advanced long-range rifles, often with telescopic sights. They were frequently seen as the standard-setters for light infantry, utilising the cover and terrain, and their reputation for skill in field craft, self-assuredness and discipline lives on to this day.

Despite Berdan's obvious contribution to the Union army during the war, and the fact that he was admired so greatly by General Winfield Scott, he is not, by many, regarded as one of the best commanders. He is reported as having been an aggressive and crusty man, and Major Dyer of the Soringfield Armory is quoted as having considered him to be 'thoroughly unscrupulous and unreliable'. Although he was considered to be a crack marksman, it is said that he was thought by many to be unfit for command.

Berdan resigned on 2 January 1864 and continued his career of invention, subsequently inventing numerous engines of war. He died on 31 March 1893, and is buried in Section 2 of Arlington National Cemetery.

CONFEDERATE
Boyd, Maria Isabella (Belle) (1843–1900)

Belle Boyd was born in Martinsburg, then Virginia, now West Virginia, in the Shenandoah Valley on 9 May 1843. She was the daughter of Ben Boyd and she attended Mount Washington Female College in Baltimore, Maryland.

When war broke out in 1861, Belle, who was a dedicated lover of the South, began fund-raising activities on behalf of the Confederates. When her home town of Martinsburg became occupied by Union troops (July 1861), Belle began her career

(Library of Congress)

as a spy. She would regularly glean information from the Union troops using her feminine ways, and then pass it on to the Confederate authorities. Belle and her mother protected their house from Union troops, and when one soldier attempted to gain access to their home in order to raise the Union flag, Belle shot him dead. She was tried but acquitted of murder, her defence counsel managing to obtain a verdict of justifiable homicide.

Belle was a constant provider of information to 'Stonewall' Jackson, often travelling through dangerous terrain in order to get the intelligence to him. She also served as a courier and scout with J.S. Mosby's guerrillas, and has become known as one of the most famous Confederate spies.

She was arrested during the campaigns in the valley (1862), and again twice in 1863, when she was first exchanged and

on the second occasion was released because of typhoid. In 1864 she sailed on a blockade runner to England bearing letters from Confederate President Jefferson Davis. It was during this journey that she met her future husband, Sam Hardinge, a Union sailor. After some persuasion from Belle, Hardinge allowed the Confederate captain of the ship to escape. Hardinge was court-martialled and discharged from the navy, and the two married in England in August 1864.

Belle Boyd Hardinge then commenced her second career, that of an actress, touring both England and America, retiring in 1886. Because of financial difficulties she then commenced life as a lecturer, giving talks about her own life and exploits. She died on one of these tours in Kilbourn, Wisconsin, on 11 June 1900 of a heart attack.

9

(Library of Congress)

Braxton Bragg was born on 22 March 1817 in Warren County, North Carolina, and was the brother of Confederate Attorney-General Thomas Bragg. He attended West Point (United States Military Academy) in 1837 and graduated as fifth in the class. After graduation he received his lieutenancy in the artillery, serving in Florida during the Seminole Wars. From 1843 to 1845 Bragg served in garrison at Fort Moultrie and fought in the occupation of Texas. He was breveted captain as a result of his gallant service in the war with Mexico, major for valour at Monterey and lieutenant-colonel for his actions at Buena Vista.

In June 1846 he was promoted to captain, 3rd Artillery, under General Gaines, but declined promotion to major of 1st Cavalry and resigned from service in 1856. Braxton Bragg had gained a reputation as a strict disciplinarian who had an unblemished and distinguished military career.

In 1861, at the outbreak of war, Braxton Bragg was placed in command of the Army of Louisiana and commissioned to brigadier-general, commanding troops at Pensacola, and being responsible for maintaining the defences.

During 1862 Bragg was involved in the battles of Corinth and Shiloh. The battle of Shiloh is remembered as the combat in which Albert Sidney Johnston was replaced by Pierre Beauregard. Braxton Bragg was promoted to general and given command of the Army of the Mississippi, with Polk, Hardee and Breckinridge as his corps commanders, and when Beauregard was removed from duty, possibly due to his poor relationship with Jefferson Davis, Braxton Bragg took over his command. This gave Braxton Bragg command of all troops and forces between the Mississippi river and Atlanta, with the exception of the east Tennessee area, which remained under the command of General Kirby Smith.

Throughout this command Bragg was paramount in the campaigns around Kentucky, Chattanooga, Munfordville, Bardstown and Lexington. He was victorious at Perryville against Don Carlos Buell, and moved his troops from there back to Knoxville. From Knoxville Bragg then began his move into Middle Tennessee, reaching Murfreesboro on 26 November 1862. At the end of December Bragg's troops were victorious in fending off an advance of Rosecrans's army, but were repulsed and forced to retreat to Tullahoma at the start of the New Year.

June 1863 found Braxton Bragg in Chattanooga, but by September the Confederates had fallen back into Georgia, and Bragg fought in the battle of Chickamauga, defeating Rosecrans. As a result of this victory Bragg then fell upon the beaten Union army at Chattanooga whilst Longstreet hit Knoxville. Unfortunately for Bragg and the rest of the Confederate army, the now weakened and virtually starving Union troops were reinforced by

Grant, forcing Bragg to retire from Missionary Ridge.

For a short spell in 1864 Braxton Bragg was removed from command in the battlefield and was appointed as advisor to Jefferson Davis on the conduct of the military operations of the Confederates, being based in Richmond. However, it was considered that he was ineffective in this position, and in November of that year he was given command of the Department of North Carolina. In January 1865 Bragg commanded the army at Wilmington, and in the final stages of the war he fought at the battle of Bentonville. When Joseph E. Johnston took over his command, Braxton Bragg was given the role of supervisor of Hoke's division, and whilst in this role he surrendered at Durham Station.

After the Appomattox Court House surrender Bragg travelled through South Carolina and into Georgia with Jefferson Davis. Bragg had lost all his property and possessions as a result of the war, but he gained a position as a civil engineer in New Orleans, and eventually became the superintendent of operations to improve the harbour at Mobile, Alabama.

It has been said of Braxton Bragg that he was:

an officer of remarkable industry and conscientiousness and unspotted character. He never praised others nor allowed himself to be flattered. His devotion to duty led him to neglect those amenities of social life which are valuable even in war, and he suffered in consequence, but no one ever questioned his patriotism, or his courage.

Finally settling in Galveston, Texas, Braxton Bragg died on 27 September 1876 whilst walking down the street with a friend. He is buried in Mobile, Alabama.

Braxton Bragg's headquarters on Missionary Ridge, Tennessee. (Library of Congress)

Brown, John (1800–59)

Despite the fact that John Brown had died before the outbreak of the American Civil War, his actions and beliefs had been paramount in causing the unrest that led to the war itself.

John Brown was born in Connecticut on 9 May 1800, and he spent much of his early life in Ohio. In 1825 he and his wife, Dianthe, together with their seven children, moved to Pennsylvania. Dianthe died in 1831, and the following year John Brown married 16-year-old Mary Anne Day, who bore him a further thirteen children. They had a difficult life, with little money, and John Brown often spent his leisure time in the company of African-Americans, particularly in the two years he lived in a freedmen's community in North Elba. Brown had a vision about slave uprisings and racism, and became a militant abolitionist, organising a self-protection league for freed and fugitive slaves.

In 1855 he travelled, together with several young people, including some of his sons, to Kansas to help make the state a haven for anti-slavery settlers. In 1856, again in the company of some of his sons, Brown visited the homes of pro-slavery people at Pottawatomie Creek, dragging the householders from their homes and killing them. From this point John Brown became known as 'Old Brown of Osawatomie'. He then returned to Ohio, but carried out two more trips to Kansas with the purpose of freeing slaves throughout the south. Several New England abolitionists supported Brown financially, and he continued his mission throughout Missouri.

By 1859 Brown had moved into western Virginia, and on 16 October he and his followers raided the armoury and arsenal at Harper's Ferry. His plan was to arm his followers, but he was thwarted when the

(Library of Congress)

US Marines under brevet Colonel Robert E. Lee trapped the men and stormed the building. Ten of Brown's men were killed, and eight, including Brown, were taken prisoner.

John Brown was tried and found guilty of treason against Virginia. He was hanged at Charlestown on 2 December 1859, and it was reported that 'the stately, fearless, unrepentant manner in which he comported himself in court and on the gallows made him a martyr in parts of the north'.

(Library of Congress)

Susquehanna in the Perry expedition to Japan, was promoted to captain in 1855 and was the Commandant of the Washington Navy Yard between 1859 and 1861.

With the outbreak of war, Buchanan was certain that Maryland would leave the Union states, and he promptly resigned his commission. However, when Maryland did not secede he attempted to withdraw this, but was instead dismissed from the service in May 1861 and joined the Confederate navy, where he received a captain's commission in September that year, having spent a number of years gaining experience and travelling the world extensively for the Union navy.

Buchanan was placed in command of the defences on the James river, Virginia, and he led the ironclad *Virginia* in Hampton Roads on 8 March 1862. This was a successful attack on the Union warships *Cumberland* and *Congress*, but Buchanan was wounded during the action and had to be taken off the *Virginia*.

By August of the same year Buchanan had recovered from his injuries and was promoted to the rank of admiral. He was sent to command the Confederate naval forces in Mobile Bay, Alabama, where he was responsible for overseeing the construction of the ironclad *Tennessee*.

On 5 August 1864 Buchanan was on board the *Tennessee* during the battle with the Union fleet under the command of Rear-Admiral David Glasgow Farragut. Buchanan was wounded and taken prisoner during this conflict, and remained a prisoner until February 1865, when he was exchanged. He was still recovering from the injuries sustained during the conflict when the war ended.

Franklin Buchanan died on 11 May 1874 in his native Maryland, having moved back there when he retired from his work as a businessman in Mobile from the end of the war until 1870.

Franklin Buchanan was born on 13 September 1800 in Baltimore, Maryland. He joined the US navy as a midshipman in 1815, being promoted to lieutenant in 1825 and to commander in 1841, during which time he commanded the *Vincennes* and *Germantown*. Between 1845 and 1847 Franklin Buchanan was the first Superintendent of the US Naval Academy and also served in the Mexican War. During the 1850s he commanded the steam frigate

13

(Library of Congress)

As Commander of the State Guard of Kentucky at the outbreak of war, Buckner issued an address to the state urging them to take up arms against Abraham Lincoln's forces. He resigned his post on 20 July 1861, and in September of that year was made Brigadier-General of the Confederate army, initially commanding in central Kentucky. It was from here that he led a division to reinforce Confederate troops at the battle of Fort Donelson, where Grant demanded an unconditional surrender in February 1862. Buckner was taken prisoner after the surrender, but was exchanged six months later, on 27 August.

Buckner was then promoted to major-general, and led his division in the battle of Perryville before he moved to take over, firstly, command of the Gulf Coast and then the Department of East Tennessee.

Buckner, despite some ill-feelings resulting from the transfer of his command to Braxton Bragg, reinforced Bragg and his command in the battle of Chickamauga. He was returned to east Tennessee just before Chattanooga, and served under Longstreet there during the siege of Knoxville.

Because of his love for poetry, Buckner acquired the nickname 'Simon the Poet', particularly during 1864 and his time in Richmond. Buckner finally surrendered to General Kirby Smith at the battle of Baton Rouge on 26 May 1865.

Simon Bolivar Buckner was born on 1 April 1823 in Hart County, Kentucky. He graduated from West Point in 1844 and entered the 2nd Infantry, serving with them in Mexico, winning two brevets and suffering a wound at Churubusco. In the years running up to the war, Buckner was a businessman, organiser and Commander of the Kentucky State Guard and Adjutant-General of the Illinois militia, when he supervised the reorganisation of Kentucky's armed forces, and the construction of the Chicago custom house. He was also a prominent member of the Knights of the Golden Circle in Kentucky.

After the war Buckner was forced to remain in New Orleans, but finally, after serving as a pallbearer at General Grant's funeral, he returned to Kentucky, serving as governor and running for the vice-presidency (1896). He died on 8 January 1914 in Mundfordville, Kentucky, the only surviving Confederate officer over the rank of brigadier-general.

(Library of Congress)

office and as a lieutenant-colonel working as an adjutant of the Department of the Pacific.

On 17 May 1861 Buell was appointed brigadier-general of volunteers, assisting McClellan to form the Army of the Potomac and later helping in the organisation of the Army of the Ohio. He was promoted to major-general of volunteers in March 1862 and was involved in the battle of Nashville. This involvement at Nashville, despite the fact that the capital was taken with little opposition, was undertaken against the opinions of both Abraham Lincoln and McClellan.

From Nashville Buell moved to support General Grant at the Pittsburg Landing on the Tennessee river, then was involved in the conflicts at Shiloh, Corinth, and Chattanooga. The Union authorities, who were not satisfied with the progress being made by Buell, then instructed him to hand over his command to George H. Thomas in September 1862, but this was soon revoked, and by 8 October Buell became involved in the battle of Perryville. He failed, however, to pursue the retreating Confederate force during this battle, and he was relieved of his duties on 24 October, when he was replaced by Rosecrans. Buell claimed that he had failed to advance because of his lack of supplies and lack of orders. He returned to Indianapolis to await the decision of the authorities, but when the decision arrived on 23 May 1864, Buell resigned his commission within a few days.

After the war ended, Buell became engaged in the coal-mining industry, and became president of the Green River Iron Company. He was also employed as a government pension agent between 1885 and 1889. Buell died on 19 November 1898 at his home near Paradise, Kentucky, and he was buried in Bellefontaine Cemetery in St Louis, Missouri.

Don Carlos Buell was born near Marietta, Ohio, on 23 March 1818, although he spent most of his early years living with an uncle in Lawrenceburg, Indiana. He graduated from West Point in 1841 and served as company officer of infantry during the Seminole and Mexican Wars. He spent the years running up to the war in the Adjutant-General's

Bronze statue of John Buford. (Lisa Mattson)

John Buford was born on 4 March 1826 in Woodford County, Kentucky, but after the death of his mother (Anne Bannister) the following year, Buford, his father (John Buford Sr) and brother (Napoleon Bonaparte Buford) moved to Stephenson (now known as Rock Island), Illinois. He graduated sixteenth out of thirty-eight from West Point in 1848, serving in the dragoons, and was involved along the frontier and in the expedition against the Mormons in Utah (1857–8).

In 1861 Buford's regiment marched from Kansas to Washington, DC, where he undertook staff duty and then a position on Major-General John Pope's staff in northern Virginia until he was made a brigadier-general and appointed General McClellan's Chief of Cavalry during the Maryland Campaign. Whilst leading his brigade of cavalry at Second Bull Run (1862) Buford sustained a wound, but by the spring of 1863 he was in command of the Reserve Brigade, composed predominantly of regular army units. This brigade, under Buford's command, fought at the battle of Fredericksburg, and took part in Stoneman's raid in the battle of Chancellorsville and in the conflicts at Brandy Station, Aide, Middleburg and Upperville.

Buford also led his troops at the battle of Gettysburg (1863) and was successful in holding off the Confederate forces by securing McPherson's Bridge for enough time to allow the Union troops to establish a defence position. This enabled Meade to make a stand south and east of the town of Gettysburg over the following few days. Buford also served through the Bristoe Campaign during 1863, but in August of that year he was allowed leave to return home to Georgetown, Kentucky, where his daughter had recently died. When Buford returned to the battlefield, he, too, was taken ill, and finally he had to relinquish his command on 21 November 1863.

John Buford died of typhoid fever on 16 December 1863. His commission as major-general of volunteers, dated from 1 July 1863, was presented to him shortly before he died. He is buried at West Point, and it is believed that his concepts of using horses to transport troops and to use cavalry in scouting were an integral part of the success of the Union army in a number of conflicts.

(Library of Congress)

A mbrose Everett Burnside was born on 23 May 1824 in Liberty, Indiana. He graduated from West Point in 1847, serving in the Mexican War as a lieutenant of artillery, but resigned his commission in 1853. During his non-military years, Burnside invented and manufactured a breechloading rifle and served on the Illinois Central Railroad.

At the outbreak of war Burnside was asked by the Governor of Rhode Island to organise and lead a regiment of volunteers, which he did, and after successfully leading this regiment at First Bull Run (July 1861) he was promoted to brigadier-general.

After Burnside's involvement in the battle of Antietam (September 1862), he was instructed, by Abraham Lincoln, to replace George McClellan (a family friend of Burnside) as commander of the Army of the Potomac. It was at the battle of Antietam that Burnside fought to hold the stone bridge which is now known as 'Burnside Bridge'. Under this reluctant command, Burnside, together with Joseph Hooker, Edwin Summer and William Franklin, launched into battle at Fredericksburg (December). This was not a success for Burnside, with losses of over 12,000, and he was swiftly replaced as commander of the Army of the Potomac by Joseph Hooker.

Burnside was given command of the Army of the Ohio in March of the following year, and whilst in this role he had slightly more success. Burnside succeeded in capturing Morgan's Raiders, and was praised for his performance at the siege of Knoxville. He returned to the east to become involved in the Wilderness Campaign, and then took part in organising a regiment of Pennsylvania coal-miners to construct tunnels and place dynamite throughout the front lines at Petersburg. Burnside, commanding a corps under Generals Meade and Grant during the siege of Petersburg (1864), had further failure here. The explosions created a huge crater, which Burnside's troops inexplicably charged into, leaving them at the mercy of the Confederate troops. This incident became known as 'the Battle of the Crater', and virtually marked the end of Burnside's military career. Burnside resigned in April 1865, was elected a US Senator for Rhode Island in 1874. He died at Bristol, Rhode Island, on 13 September 1881. Burnside's distinctive, bushy whiskers were known throughout the country as 'sideburns'. 17

(Library of Congress)

leading the regiment as its colonel. The 12th New York were the first to cross the Long Bridge into Virginia after the secession. Butterfield was later to command a brigade of Patterson's army, and was to be given a commission as brigadier and major-general of volunteers and took command of a division of the 5th Corps. Butterfield fought at First Bull Run (July 1861) and was awarded a Congressional Medal of Honor (awarded in 1892) for the carrying of the flag of the 3rd Pennsylvania at Gaines's Mill, where he was wounded (27 June 1862).

During Second Bull Run Butterfield commanded successfully, as he did at Antietam and Fredericksburg, where he was involved in the charges on Marye's Heights. He was then promoted to major-general of volunteers (November), and during the battles of Chancellorsville and Gettysburg was Chief of Staff to Generals Hooker and Meade, being wounded for a second time when a piece of shell struck him. Having recovered from his injuries, Butterfield returned to duty in late 1863, joining Hooker at Chattanooga. During the Atlanta Campaign Butterfield was given a division to command, but once again ill-health took over and he was forced to retire from the battlefield, taking on the post of recruiting officer in New York.

Butterfield continued his recruiting duties after the war until 1870, when he retired from his post to resume his business interests.

He died in Cold Spring, New York, on 17 July 1901, and is credited with having the most ornate tomb in the West Point grounds. He is also credited with the writing of 'Taps', the distinctive bugle call, with the help of his bugler, O.W. Norton, as well as with being responsible for the implementation of corps identification badges.

Daniel Adams Butterfield was born on 31 October 1831 in Utica, New York, the son of John Butterfield of the Overland Mail Company. After graduating from Union College, Butterfield studied law and travelled to the south with the American Express Company.

When war broke out in 1861, Butterfield was enrolled as a sergeant in the Washington, DC militia. Very soon, however, he 18 transferred to the 12th New York militia,

W illiam Carney was born into slavery in Norfolk, Virginia, but during his teenage years he and his father escaped to the north and bought their family's freedom. They settled in New Bedford, Massachusetts.

In early 1863 the Union army called for African-American volunteers, and William Carney, at the age of 23 years, enlisted in the Morgan Guards on 17 February 1863. During the spring Carney's company was merged with others to become part of the 54th Massachusetts Volunteer Infantry Regiment. When asked at the time why he had volunteered, Carney told the *Liberator* newspaper:

Previous to the formation of colored troops, I had a strong inclination to prepare myself for the ministry; but when the country called for persons, I could best serve my God serving my country and my oppressed brothers.

Together with 46 other African-American volunteers of Company C, 54th Massachusetts, Carney fought at the battle of Fort Wagner, South Carolina on 18 July 1863, one of the 'bloodiest battles of the war'. The regiment was commanded by Colonel Robert Gould Shaw, who was wounded just as the troops reached the summit of the fort. Carney was also wounded in the head, leg and hip, and he fell very close to Shaw.

When Carney noticed that the soldier who carried the flag had been wounded, he pulled himself to his feet and took the flag from the colour sergeant. Carrying the flag aloft through a volley of enemy bullets across the battlefield, which was strewn with his dead and wounded comrades, and despite his agonies, Carney delivered the flag to a member of his own regiment. Amidst cheers Carney shouted:

(Library of Congress)

'Boys, the old flag never touched the ground!'

Carney then fell to the ground. For his brave and selfless heroic efforts William Carney became the first African-American Congressional Medal of Honor recipient (issued 23 May 1900).

Carney was mustered out of the army in 1864 and returned to New Bedford. He became employed as a letter carrier, finally retiring in 1901. He regularly led the Memorial Day parades, including the 1904 one when he was orator at the Shaw Monument on Boston Common, and he was a popular speaker at patriotic events.

Lawrence Joshua Chamberlain was born in Brewer, Maine, on 8 September 1828 in a cottage near his family's homestead. In 1848 he entered Bowdoin College, Brunswick, and began using Joshua as his first name. He was later to become a professor at the college.

In August 1862 Chamberlain entered the war as Lieutenant-Colonel of the 20th Regiment of Maine Volunteers. With his regiment Chamberlain fought in the battles of Antietam (September 1862), Shepherdstown Ford, Fredericksburg (December 1862) and Chancellorsville (April 1863). He was wounded at Fredericksburg, but by the battle of Gettysburg, where he was again wounded (July 1863) he had been given command of the regiment, and for his action at Little Round Top he was awarded the Congressional Medal of Honor.

Chamberlain commanding the 20th Regiment of Maine Volunteers at Gettysburg. (Tim Hall)

By November 1863 Chamberlain was suffering from malaria, and was relieved of his field service and sent to Washington to carry out lighter duties. However, he resumed command of the regiment in May 1864, leading the troops in the battle of Cold Harbor and being assigned the brigade command the following month. At Petersburg Chamberlain was wounded to such an extent that he was not expected to live, and he was promoted on the battlefield to brigadier-general by General Grant. His wounds were very serious, but Chamberlain returned to the battlefield and was wounded for a fourth time at Petersburg. Despite his numerous injuries, he also took part in the Appomattox

(Library of Congress)

Campaign, and was given command of the troops who formally accepted the surrender of the Confederate army.

After the war Chamberlain returned to Bowdoin College as a professor, and was elected Governor of Maine. He became President of Bowdoin and was named a US Surveyor of Customs at the Port of Portland, Maine.

Joshua Chamberlain also wrote a number of books about his wartime experiences, including *The Passing of the Armies*, *My Story of Gettysburg* and *Through Blood and Fire at Gettysburg*. He finally died, it is said as a direct result of the injuries sustained during the war, on 24 February 1914, at the age of 86. He was buried at Pine Grove Cemetery in Brunswick, Maine.

CONFEDERATE
Cheatham, Benjamin Franklin (1820–86)

Benjamin Franklin Cheatham was born in the city of Nashville on 20 October 1820 to a farming family. He served as a captain in the 1st Tennessee and as Colonel of the 3rd Tennessee during the Mexican War. He was active in the state militia and was one of its senior officers before the outbreak of war, having already gained a reputation as being an excellent fighter who showed a high regard for his men.

On 9 May 1861 Cheatham was appointed as Major-General of the provisional Army of Tennessee, but by July had been promoted to Brigadier-General of the Confederate States Army.

Cheatham led a division at Belmont, where he led three regiments of Pillow's force and was promoted to major-general on 10 March 1862 before he was wounded at the battle of Shiloh. He was also involved in the fighting at Corinth (October 1862), Perryville (October 1862), Chickamauga, Murfreesboro (December 1862), the Tullahoma Campaign, and the Atlanta Campaign. At Murfreesboro Cheatham's division was one of four which drove back the Union troops a distance of between three and four miles. At Kennesaw Mountain and around Atlanta, Cheatham's division, together with that of Patrick Cleburne, inflicted severe casualties on the Union troops, as well as capturing a number of artillery pieces belonging to the Union army.

Cheatham became involved in the disagreements between Braxton Bragg and William J. Hardee during the invasion of

(Library of Congress)

Middle Tennessee, finally taking command of Hardee's corps when he left the army. Cheatham then went on to fight at Nashville and to the Carolinas in April 1865 until the Confederate surrender at Durham Station.

At the end of the war General Grant offered Cheatham an appointment in the civil service, but he declined, choosing to return to his farm and to spend the next four years as a superintendent of the State prison. In 1885 Benjamin Cheatham became a postmaster at Nashville and he held this position until his death at the age of 66 on 4 September 1886. His funeral, attended by a vast number of people, was said to have been the most imposing ever held in Nashville.

21

Patrick Ronayne Cleburne was born in County Cork, Ireland, on St Patrick's Day (17 March) 1828. He joined the British army in the 41st Regiment of Foot as a private in 1850, remaining there until 1853, when he left the army as a corporal and emigrated to America. He ultimately settled in Arkansas, and by 1861 he had an established career as a successful property attorney in Helena.

Cleburne was one of the first to join the Confederates, as a captain in the 1st Arkansas (later known as the 15th Arkansas Regiment), and was elected as colonel of the regiment that he had helped to form. He was then transferred, along with William J. Hardee, to central Kentucky, and was promoted to brigadier-general (4 March 1862). Cleburne fought at the battles of Shiloh and Corinth, in the Kentucky Campaign, and at Richmond, Perryville, Murfreesboro and Chickamauga. He was wounded at both Richmond and Perryville, but by the time he reached Murfreesboro he had been promoted to major-general (13 December 1862). He defeated Sherman at the battle of Missionary Ridge, where he was in command of the tunnel; and he was responsible for capturing hundreds of Union prisoners. He commanded firstly his division and ultimately the corps throughout the Atlanta Campaign, where he was successful at Pickett's Mill over Howard's corps of Sherman's army and then moved with Hood into Middle Tennessee.

(Library of Congress)

At the battle of Franklin (20 November 1864), Patrick Cleburne, who became known as the 'Stonewall Jackson of the West' was killed on the battlefield. He was the most senior general of the six killed to die in this disastrous battle for the Confederacy. His death was considered to be a terrible blow for the Army of Tennessee, exceeded only by the death of 'Stonewall' Jackson. He was buried near Franklin, but his remains were later transferred to Helena, Arkansas.

Cleburne was credited with the proposal that slaves should be recruited into the Confederate army for military service in exchange for their freedom. This was rejected at the time by the Richmond authorities, but was passed by the Confederate Congress shortly after Cleburne's death and within weeks of the fall of the Confederacy.

Clem, John 'Johnny' Lincoln (1851–1937)

Johnny Lincoln Clem was born in Newark, Ohio, on 13 August 1851. At the outbreak of war Johnny was 9 years old. He ran away from home in May 1861 with the intention of joining the army.

After firstly applying to the commander of the 3rd Ohio Regiment and being turned down because 'we don't enlist infants', Johnny sought out the 22nd Michigan, only to be given a similar answer. However, despite this rejection, and with a determined will, Johnny decided that he would follow the regiment and wear down their resistance. This appeared to work, because Johnny became the regiment's drummer boy.

Despite the fact that Johnny had never officially enlisted, he performed regular camp duties, acted as drummer and was paid an enlisted soldier's pay of $13 a month, which was donated to him by the officers of the regiment.

In April 1862, at the battle of Shiloh, Johnny's drum was hit by artillery fire and his fame as 'Johnny Shiloh' began. In September 1863, at the battle of Chickamauga Johnny was wielding a musket that had been trimmed to his size by his comrades. Whilst riding a caisson at the front of the action Johnny was confronted by a Confederate officer, who shouted, 'Surrender, you damned little Yankee!' Johnny's response was to kill the Confederate officer, and as a result of this action, he won national attention and became known as the 'Drummer Boy of Chickamauga'.

(Library of Congress)

Johnny remained with the Union army throughout the remainder of the war. He was wounded twice and eventually was formally enrolled in the army and received his own pay for his service as a courier.

When the war ended Johnny Clem applied to enter West Point, but was refused because it was considered that he lacked suitable education. Determinedly Johnny was again not to be beaten, and he applied directly to President Ulysses S. Grant, who had been his general at Shiloh. Grant allowed Johnny Clem to join the regular army on 18 December 1871 as a lieutenant, and he remained in post until 1903, when he was promoted to colonel and assistant quartermaster-general. Johnny Clem retired from the army as a major-general in 1916, and died at San Antonio, Texas, on 13 May 1937.

23

George Armstrong Custer was born in New Rumley, Harrison County, Ohio, on 5 December 1839. He trained as a teacher and taught until he entered West Point (United States Military Academy), from which he graduated last in his class in June 1861. On leaving West Point as an unpopular character, he was commissioned a second lieutenant in the 2nd Cavalry (later to become the 5th Cavalry) on 24 June 1861.

George Custer spent the first part of the American Civil War as a courier and staff officer. During First Bull Run (1861) he carried despatches and served on the staff of McClellan and Pleasanton. After distinguished action at Aldie (June 1863), he was promoted firstly to captain and then to brigadier-general of volunteers, being in command of the 2nd battalion, 3rd division, Cavalry Corps. In this role he was given command of the Michigan 'Wolverines' cavalry brigade fighting at the battle of Gettysburg (July 1863). This command assisted in the defeat of J.E.B. Stuart's attempts to make a cavalry strike behind the Union lines, and contributed to the victory of the Army of the Potomac. In the Shenandoah Valley Campaign Custer commanded the 3rd Cavalry Division and was involved at Fisher's Hill and Five Forks. His command was responsible for cutting off the Confederate army's last escape route at Appomattox in April 1865, and he was promoted to major-general of volunteers and breveted major-general in the regular army.

From July 1863 George Custer and his various commands participated in virtually every cavalry action in Virginia until the Confederate surrender in April 1865.

When the army was reorganised in 1868, Custer was appointed Lieutenant-Colonel

of the 7th US Cavalry. In 1874 he led his troops to investigate rumours of gold in South Dakota's Black Hills. This action, it is considered, led to the fighting in the various actions against the Western Indians, whose sacred grounds had been violated. His life and military career ended at his famous 'Last Stand' on 25 June 1876 when he died at the battle of the Little Big Horn, along with the majority of his regiment and his own brother, Thomas Ward Custer.

(Library of Congress)

24

Thomas Ward Custer was born on 15 March 1845, in New Rumley, Harrison County, Ohio, a younger brother of George Armstrong Custer. Although Thomas Custer was two years younger than the required age for enlistment, when war broke out he enlisted, at the age of 16. He entered his military career as a private in Company H, 21st Ohio, on 2 September 1861.

During the first years of the war Thomas Custer saw action at Stone's River, Chickamauga, Chattanooga and in the Atlanta Campaign, but was mustered out of the army after he had completed his three-year service in October 1864.

The following month saw Thomas Custer re-enlisted as a second lieutenant in the 6th Michigan Cavalry, and he was assigned to the staff of his brother's division in the Shenandoah Valley, moving with him to Petersburg and then Appomattox.

Days before the end of the war Thomas Custer was awarded the Medal of Honor for his action in the fight at Namozine Church, where he captured the flag of a Confederate division. Three days later he received a second commendation for heroic actions whilst capturing the colours at the battle of Sayler's Creek, resulting in another Congressional Medal of Honor. According to General Sheridan's later writings:

Thomas Custer leaped his horse over the enemy's works, being one of the first to enter them, and captured two stand of colors, having his horse shot under him and received a severe wound.

Lieutenant Custer had been seriously wounded in the face, and it is said that he had to be placed under arrest by General Custer, his brother, in order to stop him from continuing the fighting and to allow him to receive the necessary medical attention. Thomas Custer was breveted through major-of-volunteers and lieutenant-colonel in the regular army.

When the war ended, Thomas Custer was commissioned into the regular army and joined the 7th Cavalry, his brother's regiment. He died at the battle of the Little Big Horn on 25 June 1876, alongside his more famous brother, being the only soldier to win two Congressional Medals of Honor during the American Civil War.

Custer crossing Dakota territory, 1874. (National Archive)

Jubal Anderson Early was born in Franklin County, Virginia, on 3 November 1816. He graduated from West Point in 1837 and was promoted to first lieutenant of artillery the following year, but he resigned in order to practise law in Virginia. From 1841 to 1842 Early was involved in State legislature, and from 1842 to 1852 he was Commonwealth Attorney, this service being broken for a short period between 1847 and 48 when he served in the Mexican War as Major of the Virginia Volunteers.

Early was opposed to secession at first, but was a member of the Virginia convention formed to assess the position of the State, and was soon convinced and enthused enough to become commissioned as Colonel of the 24th Regiment of Virginia Infantry. He commanded a brigade at Blackburn's Ford, and after successful actions at First Bull Run (1861) he was promoted to brigadier-general. He was wounded at Williamsburg (May

1862), where he led the charge of his brigade, and at Second Bull Run (August 1862) he commanded a brigade of Ewell's division of Jackson's corps.

After General Lawton was wounded at Sharpsburg, Early took command of Ewell's division against the Union attacks at Sharpsburg. By January 1863 Early had been promoted to major-general, and whilst the Chancellorsville Campaign was raging, he held the heights of Fredericksburg, leading his own men and those of Barksdale against Sedgwick's corps. He was then detached and took over command in the Shenandoah during the winter of 1863–4.

During the Pennsylvania Campaign Early was paramount in the attack on Winchester, capturing some 4,000 Union troops, and from here he marched to Harrisburg, via York, being recalled, soon after he had reached the Susquehanna river, to Gettysburg, where he was involved in the first two days of fighting.

Early was involved in the opening battle of the Wilderness Campaign whilst in temporary command of Hill's corps, and met and defeated Burnside at Spotsylvania Court House and then at Bethesda Church during the battle of Cold Harbor, directing his operations at the North Anna and attacking Grant's right flank.

By May 1864 Early had been promoted to lieutenant-general and had moved to Lynchburg to defend the Confederate rear, marching from there through the Shenandoah Valley and into Maryland, fighting and defeating Wallace at Monocacy and continuing on to the outskirts of Washington. Early had intended to assault the defences at Washington with his 8,000 men, but when the Union forces were reinforced by Sheridan, he was forced to fall back into the valley. Here he began actively to injure and inhibit the Union communications. In September and October of 1864 Early was

(Library of Congress)

defeated in a series of battles against Sheridan at Winchester (3rd battle), Fisher's Hill and Cedar Creek. Early established his army at New Market, and Sheridan retired from the valley and fell back to Staunton, but his corps was recalled in December.

In March 1865 Early's force was destroyed at Waynesborough, and he was removed by General Robert E. Lee. Lee had to relieve Early of command after his defeat by Sheridan because Lee could not defend his general from the public condemnation without revealing how little the Confederacy had to work with.

It is said that Early rode on horseback to Texas, hoping that he would come across a Confederate force that had not surrendered, but when he could find none, he continued on to Mexico and from there sailed to Canada, fleeing both his country and the war.

After the war ended Early returned from Canada to Virginia and resumed his law practice there. Over the following years he became connected with the Louisiana Lottery and was elected as president of the Southern Historical Society.

Jubal Early was described as being an irascible officer and one of the more aggressive Confederate generals, who was a heavy drinker with an abrasive tongue, but his men were quite fond of their colourful commander, and called him 'Old Jube' or 'Old Jubilee'.

Even after the conflict had ended, Early remained 'unreconstructed' and bitter over the South's defeat until his death. He went on to wage a literary war with his fellow Confederate corps commander and Republican convert, James Longstreet. In his later years Early lived in New Orleans, but died in Lynchburg, Virginia on 2 March 1894.

UNION
Edmonds, Sarah Emma Evelyn (1841–98)

Sarah Emma Evelyn Edmonds was born in New Brunswick, Nova Scotia, in December 1841 to a father who wished she had been a boy. She had a difficult childhood, suffering at the hands of an aggressive and violent father, and eventually she fled her home and country to a new life in the United States of America.

When war broke out Emma was living in Flint, Michigan. She cropped her hair, bought a man's suit and took on the name of Frank Thompson in an attempt to enlist in the Union army. Finally, on 25 April 1861, she was successful and became a male nurse in the 2nd Volunteers of the US army. After completion of training in Washington, Emma, now known as Private Frank Thompson, was sent to join McClellan's campaign in Virginia, and not long after arriving she volunteered to act as a spy.

Disguised as a Confederate, Emma entered the enemy camps on a number of occasions, successfully gleaning information which was of use to McClellan. She did this successfully a total of eleven times, variously dressed as a black soldier whom she called 'Cuff', an Irish pedlar woman called Bridget O'Shea and a black laundress in the Confederate camps. Finally Emma became too sick with malaria to remain in the hospitals on the battlefields or to continue her spying work. It was impossible for her to check into one of the hospitals as Private Frank Thompson, as her true identity would be discovered. She travelled to Cairo, Illinois, and whilst there she saw the name of Private Frank Thompson posted on a list of deserters.

Knowing that her military career had ended, Emma travelled to Washington, working there until the end of the war as a 27 nurse. After the end of the war Emma wrote *Nurse and Spy in the Union Army*, a best-seller from which she gave all profits to the US War Relief Fund.

In 1867 Emma returned to Canada and married Linus Seeyle, with whom she had three sons, and then moved back to America once more. She petitioned the US War Department for a review of her case, being unhappy with her rank as deserter. Finally, on 5 July 1884, Emma, alias Frank Thompson, was granted by a special Act of Congress an honourable discharge from the army, plus a bonus and a veteran's pension of $12 per month. Emma died on 5 September 1898 in La Porte, Texas, and is buried in the military section of Washington Cemetery in Houston, Texas.

Pinkerton McClellan's secret service. (National Archive)

CONFEDERATE
Ewell, Richard Stoddert (1817–72)

Richard Stoddert Ewell was born on 8 February 1817 in Georgetown, District of Columbia, but he had spent a great deal of his younger life on his family's farm in Bristoe, Virginia, a location close to the First and Second Bull Run battles. He graduated well from West Point in 1840, and then he spent the next two decades as a company officer, serving in the 1st Dragoons during the Seminole and Mexican Wars, before resigning his captaincy on 7 May 1861 in order to join the Confederate South.

Ewell served in First Bull Run (July 1861) and was then given command of a division serving under 'Stonewall' Jackson in the successful Shenandoah Valley Campaign. Ewell fought alongside Jackson at the Seven Days battles, where he acquired a reputation as an aggressive fighter but a compassionate leader of men. They fought again at Cedar Mountain and then at Groveton (28 August 1862). During the battle of Groveton Ewell was so severely injured that his right leg had to be amputated, and eventually he had a

wooden one fitted. Whilst recovering in hospital, Ewell was nursed by his cousin, Lizinka Campbell Brown, who was said to have been one of the richest women in America at the time. He proposed to Lizinka, and the two were married on 24 May 1863.

Shortly after his marriage Ewell returned to the battlefield, and was swiftly promoted to lieutenant-general, commanding the corps that had been under the command of Stonewall Jackson before he was mortally wounded at the battle of Chancellorsville. Ewell's first task was to take on the Union troops at Winchester (2nd battle, 14 June 1863), where he won an impressive victory, being named for some time the 'New Jackson'. Ewell's troops captured more than 4,000 Union troops, 23 cannon and 300 supply wagons, a victorious outcome for the Confederates.

However, this success was short-lived for Ewell, certainly in the eyes of General Robert E. Lee. On the evening of the first day of the fighting at Gettysburg Ewell failed to carry out instructions given to him by Lee, and as a result the Confederates were defeated and had to retreat to Virginia.

A similar problem occurred later the same year during the Wilderness Campaign (June 1864). Another complication for Ewell here was a fall from his horse during battle at the Bloody Angle. During the fighting at Spotsylvania, where Ewell had become known by his men as 'Old Baldhead' one of the divisions under his command was virtually wiped out when it bore the worst of the Union onslaught. Ewell became ill and was forced to temporarily surrender his command, but General Lee had other ideas and made his removal from the area permanent, replacing him with Jubal Early. Ewell was sent to take over command of the Department of Henrico, the defence of Richmond, but was captured at Sayler's Creek on 6 April 1865 during the Confederate retreat to Appomattox. He was imprisoned in Fort Warren, Massachusetts, until 19 August 1865, and after his release he retired to Spring Hill, Tennessee, where he lived out the remainder of his life as a farmer, dying on 25 January 1872.

There are several theories about the lack of success of Ewell as Jackson's successor as commander of the 2nd Corps of the Army of Northern Virginia. Certainly Gettysburg was the beginning of the end for him, despite his long and successful military career prior to the American Civil War, and he has been blamed for the failure of the Confederates to capture Cemetery Hill on 1 July. Some considered that at the age of 47 he had become inadequate and indecisive; others claimed that his health was not good and that the continued fighting had told on him; still more believed that he had suffered severe trauma after the loss of his leg, whilst the more cynical claimed that his change in effectiveness was a direct result of his marriage to his wife. One fellow officer wrote of him in this context:

From a military point of view, the acquisition of a wife did not compensate for the loss of the leg. We were of the opinion that he was not the same soldier he had been when a whole man and a single one.

(Library of Congress)

Having been promoted to captain on Christmas Day 1861, Farnsworth was involved in Stoneman's Raid during the Chancellorsville Campaign. He became ill towards the end of 1862 and was unable to continue on the battlefield. He returned the following spring under the command of Brigadier-General Alfred Pleansanton, and by June 1863 had been promoted to brigadier, commanding the 1st Brigade, 3rd Division, Cavalry Corps, Army of the Potomac.

On 30 June, under the command of Brigadier-General Kilpatrick, Farnsworth and his division found themselves facing J.E.B. Stuart's cavalry in Hanover, Pennsylvania, some 25 miles from Gettysburg. The battle here raged all day long, with Farnsworth leading several charges. On 2 July they met again at Hunterstown, and Farnsworth joined General Custer and his brigade in an attack on the Confederate troops under the command of Brigadier-General Wade Hampton.

The following day, after the repulse of Pickett's Charge, Farnsworth's brigade received an order for a mounted charge from Brigadier-General Kilpatrick. Farnsworth protested strongly that this was a suicidal attempt, given that his cavalry would be assaulting infantry safely secured behind stone walls. But he was overruled by Kilpatrick, who challenged his honour and courage. This confrontation prompted Farnsworth to agree to lead the charge, and his small column, moving out of Bushman's Hill, were quickly repulsed and forced to ride around Slyder Farm and up the slope of Big Round Top. It was here that Farnsworth met his death at the hands of the 15th Alabama Infantry, who shot him five times, on 3 July 1863. Many still blame the goading of Brigadier-General Kilpatrick for the death of these troops and the suicidal charge that took place.

Elon John Farnsworth was born·on 30 July 1837 in a small hamlet called Green Oak, in Michigan. During his teenage years his family moved to Rockton, Illinois, and Farnsworth enrolled at the University of Michigan, although later he was expelled as a result of a drunken party. He then joined the march to Utah Territory as a civilian forage master, and remained at Camp Floyd until 1861, when he enlisted in the 8th Illinois Volunteer Cavalry, which had been formed by his uncle, John F. Farnsworth.

Forrest, Nathan Bedford (1821–77)

Nathan Bedford Forrest was born in Chapel Hill, Tennessee, on 13 July 1821 into a relatively poor family. In 1834 he moved with his family to Marshall County, Mississippi, to a small hill farm, where his father died soon after, leaving Forrest with the responsibility of providing for his mother, brothers and sisters. He amassed a large fortune over the following years, and by the outbreak of war he was the owner of a large cotton plantation, a prominent slave-trader and land speculator.

On 14 June 1861, despite having had no military training, Forrest enlisted in the Confederate army as a private in Josiah H. White's mounted rifles cavalry unit. He then obtained the authority of the governor to raise his own regiment of cavalry, Forrest's Tennessee Cavalry Battalion, at his own expense, in Louisville. These cavalry troops became involved in the battle at Fort Donelson (15 February 1862). Lieutenant-Colonel Forrest, hearing his fellow officers considering surrender to the Union forces, successfully led his cavalry and a number of infantry troops through the enemy lines in retreat.

Joining Albert Sidney Johnston at Shiloh (April 1862), Forrest's command again formed the rearguard on the retreat. Forrest was wounded but continued to fight until his troops had reached safety. He was promoted to brigadier-general (21 July 1862) after the siege of Corinth, and raised a brigade that effectively captured Murfreesboro (21 December 1862). Here he freed a garrison jail that had imprisoned local men, and demanded the unconditional surrender of the entire garrison.

Forrest's next success came when his troops captured the Union raiding column led by Abel D. Streight, but on 14 June 1862 Forrest was shot by one of his subordinates, Andrew W. Gould. Forrest, by all accounts, retaliated by using his penknife to mortally wound Gould. In the

battle of Chickamauga (September 1863) Forrest successfully commanded the cavalry of the right wing, but after having crossed swords with Braxton Bragg, his commander, he tendered his resignation. His resignation was not accepted, however, and Forrest was promoted to major-general in command of all cavalry in north Mississippi and west Tennessee. He entered west Tennessee with a small force, recruiting volunteers as he travelled and considerably enlarging his numbers.

In February 1864 Forrest's cavalry routed Generals Smith and Sherman at Okolona and Prairie Mound, and by June of the same year Forrest had captured Fort Pillow. Apparently a controversy developed after the battle at Fort Pillow concerning the massacre of the garrison. The fort contained 295 white and 262 African American soldiers, and it was claimed that they were killed after they had surrendered. After the war an official investigation discovered evidence that:

the Confederates were guilty of atrocities which included murdering most of the garrison after it surrendered, burying Negro soldiers alive, and setting fire to tents containing Federal wounded.

The date 10 June 1864 is considered to be that of Forrest's most significant battle. He, along with fewer than 3,000 men, engaged approximately 8,000 Union troops led by Major-General Samuel D. Sturgis at Brice's Crossroads. Sturgis was marching south into northern Mississippi with the intention of blocking Confederate cavalry from attacking Sherman's supply lines. This caused William Sherman serious problems during his Atlanta Campaign. From here Forrest moved, under Stephen D. Lee, to the battle of Tupelo, facing Andrew J. Smith, whom he later faced in August 1864 when he provided the cavalry force

31

The statue of Nathan Bedford Forrest, Forrest Park, Memphis, Tennessee. (Library of Congress)

for John B. Hood's invasion of Middle Tennessee. After Hood's abortive Nashville Campaign, the Confederate army as a

whole had depleted considerably and Forrest found himself incapable of stopping Wilson's raid through Alabama and Georgia during the final months of the war. When Richard Taylor surrendered, Forrest's cavalry were included.

Forrest had been ruined financially by the war years, but he resumed his plantation work and was elected president of the Selma, Marion and Memphis Railroad. He also lent his name to a group of enforcers of the Democratic Party known as the Ku Klux Klan, becoming its first Grand Wizard in May 1867. Despite his heroic and distinguished service during the war, there is a stigma still attached to him resulting from his days as a slave trader, the investigations about the incidents at Fort Pillow and his association with the Klan. Nathan Forrest died on 29 October 1877 in Memphis, where he is buried.

Gibbon, John (1827–96)

(Library of Congress)

John Gibbon was born on 20 April 1827 in Pennsylvania. After graduating from West Point in 1847 Gibbon served in the Mexican War and the 3rd Seminole Indian War in the regular army as captain of artillery. He also prepared the United States Artillery Manual of 1859, a manual

that was much used during the American Civil War. When he joined the Union army, despite the fact that three of his brothers had chosen to fight with the Confederate force, he was put in command of the 2nd Division of Major-General Winfield Hancock's 2nd Corps.

Gibbon was promoted to Brigadier-General of the 'Iron Brigade' in May 1862, and fought, playing a prominent role, at the battles of Gainesville, Second Bull Run (August 1862), Antietam (September 1862), Fredericksburg (December 1862), where he sustained his first injury, Chancellorsville (April 1863) and Gettysburg (July 1863). He was wounded for a second time at Gettysburg, but his men had stood fast once more and it is said that they were paramount in the failure of the Confederates.

After recovering from his injuries at Gettysburg, Gibbon rejoined his command in the Wilderness Campaign (1864). His

32

division sustained heavy losses, and in August 1864, at Ream's Station, Petersburg, they were severely defeated, Gibbon resigning his command. He had also fought at Spotsylvania (May 1864) and Cold Harbor (June 1864).

In January 1865 General Ord replaced General Butler, who had been relieved of his command of the Army of the James, and Major-General John Gibbon returned as commander of the 24th Corps. Gibbon described his involvement in the assault of Forts Gregg and Whitworth as being 'one of the most desperate in the war'. At Appomattox (1865) Gibbon was involved in the last shots fired in the war, and witnessed the Confederate surrender of General Robert E. Lee at the Court House. He is quoted as being 'one of the best divisional commanders of the Union Army of the Potomac'.

Gibbon remained in the army after the end of the American Civil War, serving in the war against Native American Indians on the frontier and leading the relief column that buried George Custer and his men at the Little Big Horn in 1876. He died on 6 February 1896.

UNION
Grant, (Hiram) Ulysses Simpson (1822–85)

Grant was the first son born to Jesse Root Grant and Hannah Simpson Grant on 27 April 1822 in Point Pleasant, Ohio. He was baptised Hiram Ulysses. The following year his family moved their tanning business to Georgetown, Ohio, where Grant attended, with little recognition for scholarly brilliance, a Georgetown grammar school, Maysville Seminary and the Presbyterian Academy of Ripley, Ohio. Despite his lack of academic ability, Grant became recognised as a competent rider of horses, with the ability to control even the wildest of animals.

33

In 1839 he entered West Point, only to find that his name had been registered incorrectly and that he had been enrolled as Ulysses Simpson Grant, from which point he no longer used the name Hiram. Grant, it would appear, was not particularly enamoured of West Point, and was regarding his time there as a necessity rather than a pleasure. He graduated twenty-first out of a class of thirty-nine in 1843.

After graduating, Grant was assigned to the 4th US Infantry as a brevet second lieutenant, based at Jefferson Barracks near St Louis, as there were no vacancies in the Dragoons, serving as a regimental quartermaster. It was here that he met his future wife, Julia Boggs Dent, who was the cousin of one of Grant's West Point peers. His regiment was sent to the southwest frontier for a short period in 1844 and he served in the Mexican War with distinction, being promoted to full second lieutenant on 20 September 1845, under the command of General Zachary Taylor, whom Grant greatly admired. When his regiment was transferred to the command of General Winfield Scott in 1847, Grant was promoted to first lieutenant and breveted captain. After the end of the Mexican War he was assigned to routine garrison duties at Sackett's Harbor, New York, and Detroit, Michigan, during which time he and Julia married, on 22 August 1848. In 1852 Grant's regiment was transferred to Fort Vancouver on the Columbia river under the command of Colonel Robert Buchanan, during which time Grant was promoted to full captain. On 11 April 1854, however, following a quarrel with Buchanan, Grant resigned his commission and returned to Missouri, where he attempted a farming career on his father-in-law's land for four years before finally moving to Galena, Illinois, to work as a clerk in his father's tanning business, now run by his two younger brothers. There were rumours that Grant had been drinking heavily and had been warned of possible disciplinary action by his post commander.

When the American Civil War broke out, Grant helped to organise the first company of Union volunteers in Galena, and remained in charge of mustering the new volunteers until 24 May 1861, when he was given command of the 21st Illinois Regiment. On 7 August he was appointed brigadier-general of volunteers by Abraham Lincoln, with his headquarters based in Cairo, Illinois, moving shortly afterwards to the junction of the Ohio and Tennessee rivers and making a failed assault on the Confederates at Belmont in November.

In February 1862 Grant persuaded his commanding officer, General Henry W. Halleck, to allow him to assault, with 17,000 men and a flotilla of gunboats under Commodore Andrew Hull Foote, Forts Donelson and Henry on the Cumberland and Tennessee rivers. This became the first significant victory for the Union army in the war, the 14,000 Confederates, under Brigadier-General Simon B. Buckner, surrendering to Grant on 16 February.

In April Grant moved on to the battle of Shiloh in Tennessee against the Confederate army under General Albert S. Johnston. This was to become the bloodiest battle ever fought in America, and reports vary on Grant's involvement and level of victory. It remains fact, however, that the Union army was successful in recapturing the initiative and forcing the Confederate army to retreat. Days after the battle of Shiloh, General Halleck arrived in Pittsburg, forcing Grant to be satisfied, until July, when he resumed full command of the District of West Tennessee, with being second-in-command of the army.

Grant was made Commander of the Department of Tennessee in October 1862, and began his assault on Vicksburg, Mississippi. However, after Brigadier-General William T. Sherman had been repulsed at Chickasaw Bayou and the Confederate Van Dorn had destroyed his supply base at Holly Springs, Grant had to rethink his tactics. The result was a decisive victory that eliminated by surrender the Confederate army of Lieutenant-General John C. Pemberton and cut off the trans-Mississippi states from the remainder of the Confederacy. Grant was swiftly nominated a major-general in the regular army by Abraham Lincoln as recognition, and he moved on to the battles of Chickamauga, Chattanooga, Lookout Mountain and Missionary Ridge.

Grant was called to Washington and awarded a gold medal from Congress and the personal thanks of Abraham Lincoln, and was promoted to the newly created rank of lieutenant-general commanding all the armies of the United States. With

Equestrian monument to Ulysses S. Grant in Washington DC. (John Dunnett)

his new power Grant began to compile his strategic plan of action, which involved simultaneous movements of all the Union armies in order to achieve his ultimate objective of 'unconditional surrender' of the Confederate armies. Grant accompanied General George G. Meade's Army of the Potomac into the Virginia Wilderness and at Spotsylvania Court House, on the North Anna and at Cold Harbor, but he was unsuccessful in defeating General Robert E. Lee's armies. His casualties had been enormous at these battles, and his enemies began to nickname him 'Grant the Butcher' for his apparent lack of care towards his troops.

On 12 June 1864 Grant crossed the James river and remained with the Army of the Potomac until April 1865, systematically cutting off the Confederate army's transportation lines, whilst Sheridan was achieving victories in Virginia and Sherman through Georgia. Eventually Sheridan's victory at Five Forks (1 April) forced Lee to abandon Richmond and Petersburg, and Grant cut off his retreat, finally wearing down the resistance of the Confederacy.

After the war ended, Grant was promoted to the newly created grade of full general in 1866, and in August the following year he replaced the suspended Secretary of War, Edwin M. Stanton, as interim secretary, resigning when Stanton's suspension was revoked by the Senate. In 1868 Grant stood as Republican candidate for the presidency against Horatio Seymour, and won 214 of the 294 votes.

When forming his cabinet, Grant was criticised for his selection of friends and wealthy individuals rather than strong political leaders. These inappropriate appointments led many to consider his administration to be racked with incompetence and corruption. He was not considered a successful president, and was blamed for the poor economic state of the country immediately after the war. Grant also angered many in the south with his 'Radical Reconstruction Program' which was considered by many to be the cause of terrorist organisations such as the Ku Klux Klan. However, he was re-elected to serve a second term in 1872 when the economy had improved to some extent, but despite this fact Grant was plagued with similar problems enhanced by the fact that a depression was sweeping through Europe. Grant was interested in remaining in office for a third term, but his Republican party, in 1876, enforced the tradition of a maximum two-term office and nominated Rutherford B. Hayes as their candidate.

After Grant left the presidential office in 1877 he travelled extensively with his wife, Julia, for two years. However, he then found himself in financial difficulties as he had lost the right to his military pension when he had entered politics, and at that time no pension existed for retired presidents. Apparently he was so short of money that he was forced to sell his wartime swords and souvenirs. He did, however, enter a partnership in a brokerage company called Grant and Ward, but this failed in May 1884 and he was forced to declare bankruptcy.

Grant, now suffering from throat cancer, wrote an article on the battle of Shiloh for *CenturyMagazine* in 1884, and as a result of its success began writing his memoirs about the war, *Personal Memoirs*. He sought the advice of his friend Mark Twain about the construction of this two-volume project. Grant was desperately seeking a way in which to provide for his family financially after his death. His book brought his family $450,000 in royalties, but unfortunately the author did not live to see its success or reap the benefits of the huge sales.

Ulysses S. Grant died at Mount Gregor, New York, on 23 July 1885, and his remains lie in a mausoleum on the Riverside Drive in New York City. They were finally dedicated in 1897.

Rose with one of her four daughters. (Library of Congress)

R ose O'Neal Greenhow was born on her family's farm in Tobbaco, Maryland, in 1817, but became orphaned, being brought up by her aunt in Washington. Rose's aunt kept a boarding house in the capital and mixed in the high circles of social life, claiming famous senators and military officers as friends. Rose was said to have been a beautiful and ambitious young woman with a string of suitors. She married Dr Robert Greenhow, with whom she had four daughters, but by the time war broke out Rose had been widowed.

Being well established in the Washington social scene, Rose was recruited as a Confederate spy by Colonel Thomas Jordan, Adjutant-General of the Confederate army at Manassas. He gave Rose a password and a bogus address that she could use to send him military intelligence. Rose used her contacts and feminine guiles to provide General P.G.T. Beauregard with vital information about the Union army's route and marching orders, a contribution that, according to later accounts, 'enabled the Confederate commander to win a major victory at the First Bull Run'.

She had created an espionage ring along with John C. Calhoun, but by the following month she had become a suspect and

the Union army began intercepting her messages. By the end of August 1861 Rose had been placed under house arrest, but this did not deter her from continuing her espionage. She had learned more tricks, and would often send messages wound in a ball of yarn or into the hair bun of one of her servants.

Rose was tried and imprisoned in the spring of 1862 in the Old Capital Prison, and eventually deported to Richmond, where cheering crowds greeted her when she arrived. Jefferson Davis met her in Richmond and gave her his personal thanks for her contribution to the success at First Bull Run. Davis then sent Rose to Europe, where she stayed until 1864 collecting diplomatic intelligence information. It was whilst she was returning to America, carrying urgent despatches for the Confederacy, that Rose died. The blockade runner *Condor* on which she was travelling was forced aground on 1 October 1864. Rose, having persuaded the captain to send her ashore in a lifeboat, was drowned when the boat overturned. She was buried with honours in Wilmington.

Rose's house in Washington. (Library of Congress)

37

(Library of Congress)

Wade Hampton III was born in Charleston, South Carolina, on 28 March 1818, the first son of a plantation owner and grandson of General Wade Hampton, a major-general in the American army of the revolution. He studied law and graduated at South Carolina College (1838). When war broke out Hampton was one of the richest men in the state and was serving as state senator, but resigned the post in order to join the conflict.

Hampton was wounded whilst leading the 'Hampton Legion' of the South Carolina troops at First Bull Run (1861). His services were conspicuously recognised and he was commissioned brigadier-general on 23 May 1862. In this role he commanded, and was wounded for a second time, the Confederate cavalry of the

Army of Northern Virginia in the battle of Seven Pines. Shortly afterwards he was promoted to lieutenant-general in J.E.B. Stuart's cavalry division, and was sent to command the rearguard of the Confederate army in South Carolina against General Sherman. Hampton was wounded for a third time at the battle of Gettysburg (July 1863) and promoted to major-general.

When J.E.B. Stuart died on 12 May 1884, Hampton was given his command, leading his men in a series of determined attacks, most notably the 'Beefsteak Raid' on 16 September 1864, when he captured nearly 2,500 head of cattle. Hampton was promoted to lieutenant-general in early 1865, and was involved in a series of hand-to-hand conflicts until the surrender.

The war had ruined Hampton financially, but in 1876 he was elected governor of South Carolina and was re-elected in 1878. However, he resigned on 24 February 1879 to accept a term in the United States Senate. He was re-elected in 1884 and held this office until March 1891.

Wade Hampton had been wounded seven times during the war, and also lost a leg as the result of a riding accident in his later life. He died on 11 April 1902 at the age of 84, and was buried in Trinity Churchyard, Columbia. It is reported that his final words were 'God bless all my people, black and white'.

Hancock, Winfield Scott (1824–86)

(Library of Congress)

burg (December 1862) and the battles of Marye's Heights and Chancellorsville he replaced Couch as leader of the 2nd Corps.

When John F. Reynolds died on the battlefield on the first day of the conflicts at Gettysburg, Hancock was instructed by George G. Meade to take over Reynolds's

Winfield Scott Hancock was born on 14 February 1824 in Montgomery County, Pennsylvania. He graduated from West Point in 1844 and fought in the Seminole Wars and in the infantry during the Mexican War, where he had been breveted a captain.

Hancock joined the war as a captain and assistant quartermaster, but was ordered east and promoted to brigadier-general in September 1861. He led his brigade at Williamsburg (5 May 1862), and during the battle of Antietam (September 1862) he was given command of the killed Israel B. Richardson's division of the 2nd Corps Army of the Potomac. After Fredericks-

Above and overleaf: The bronze statues of Winfield Hancock. (Lisa Mattson)

39

(Library of Congress)

When Hancock had recovered from his injury he returned to fight in the Overland and Wilderness Campaigns, and was breveted major-general in the regular army for his actions at Spotsylvania. His wound forced him to leave the army once more, and after the defeat at Ream's Station he began recruiting the 1st Veteran Volunteer Corps. In early 1865 Hancock took over command in Washington, D C, Maryland, west Virginia and the Shenandoah Valley.

Hancock was finally mustered out of the service on 26 July 1866, receiving promotion to major-general in the regular army, and he assumed command of the Department of the East based at Governor's Island, New York, in 1867. He stood as a potential Democratic candidate for the presidency in 1868, and in 1880 was the party's nominee but was defeated by James A. Garfield.

wing of the army. Showing decisive action here brought the Thanks of Congress, but Hancock was wounded in the thigh by a nail and fragments of wood and was forced to retire from the conflict in order to undertake recruiting duties.

William Hancock died at Governor's Island on 9 February 1886 whilst still in service as commander of the Department of the East, and he is buried in Montgomery Cemetery.

CONFEDERATE
Hardee, William Joseph (1815–73)

William Joseph Hardee was born in November 1815 at Camden County, Georgia. He graduated from West Point in 1838 and entered the army as a second lieutenant of the 2nd Cavalry. He was promoted to first lieutenant in 1839 and served in the Florida War (1840). Hardee was promoted to captain in 1844 and served during the Mexican War, and for his valour was breveted major. In 1853 he compiled a system of infantry tactics known as 'Hardee's Tactics' which was introduced at West Point, where he was promoted commandant as a lieutenant-colonel.

When war broke out Hardee resigned his commission and entered the Confederate army as Colonel of Cavalry at Fort

Morgan, Alabama. He was swiftly promoted to brigadier-general, and organised the brigade of Arkansas regiments, being further promoted to major-general commanding a division of the army in Kentucky and Tennessee under the command of Albert Sidney Johnston. Following the battles of Corinth (October 1862) and Shiloh, the following summer Hardee was put in command of the Army of the Mississippi, taking an active part in the battles of Perryville and Murfreesboro. He was commended by Braxton Bragg 'for skill, valour and ability'.

During 1863 Hardee was involved in the defence of Mississippi and Alabama, and the battles of Chattanooga and

Missionary Ridge, and in December he replaced Braxton Bragg in command of the army. Under Generals J.E. Johnston and J.B. Hood, Hardee commanded a corps of the army through the Atlanta Campaign, fighting at Resaca, Kennesaw Mountain, Peach Tree Creek and Jonesboro.

Towards the end of 1864 Hardee failed to stop Sherman's march to the sea, and evacuated Savannah, withdrawing into North Carolina and joining Johnston's troops at the battles of Averysboro and Bentonville, where his only son was killed in action at the age of 16. Hardee retained corps command until he surrendered, along with Johnston, on 26 April 1865.

Hardee had gained the nickname 'Old Reliable', together with a reputation for his thoroughness as a soldier who regularly inspected the arms and accoutrements of each of his soldiers. After the war he settled on an Alabama plantation. He died on 6 November 1873 at Wytheville, Virginia, and is buried at Selma, Alabama.

Fort Morgan, Mobile Point, Alabama, where Hardee entered service with the Confederate army. (National Archive)

CONFEDERATE

Heth, Henry (1825–99)

Henry Heth was born into a military family on 16 December 1825 in Chesterfield County, Virginia. He was educated at West Point and graduated last in his class of 1847 with the rank of brevet second lieutenant of the 2nd Infantry. He served in the Mexican War and was made full second lieutenant of the 8th Infantry, being promoted to first lieutenant (1853), adjutant (1854) and then captain in the 10th Infantry (1855). After being assigned to special duty in preparing target practice for the army, he then remained with the Army of Utah before resigning his Union commission to join the Confederate army as captain in April 1861.

Heth was given the responsibility of organising the quartermaster's department at Richmond, and was commissioned major, then promoted Colonel of the 45th Virginia Regiment. In this role he 41

(Library of Congress)

Giles Court House, commanded the military district at Lewisburg, and fought at Knoxville and Lexington.

In February 1863, at General Robert E. Lee's request, Heth joined the Army of Northern Virginia, commanding Field's brigade at the battle of Chancellorsville. When A.P. Hill was wounded, Heth took over his command, and after being wounded himself, was promoted major-general, leading his division through the Pennsylvania Campaign at Gettysburg, where he was also wounded and his command suffered huge losses. Following Gettysburg, Heth's division, now under the command of Pettigrew, took part in 'Pickett's Charge'.

After recovering from his wounds and being involved in the conflict at Falling Waters, Heth led his command in the battle of Bristoe Station (October 1863), Spotsylvania (May 1864), Bethesda Church (June 1864), Mine Run and the siege of Petersburg (1865). In the final months of the war Heth was involved at Ream's Station and Burgess's Mill, being briefly in corps command until finally surrendering on 9 April 1865.

After the war Heth was in the insurance business and later served the government as a surveyor and in the Office of Indian Affairs. He died on 27 September 1899 in Washington, DC.

organised General Floyd's command at Wytheville and was involved in the battles at Carnifax Ferry. In January 1862 Heth was promoted brigadier-general, and fought during that year in the battle of

CONFEDERATE
Hill, Ambrose Powell (1825–65)

Ambrose Powell Hill was born in Culpeper County, Virginia, on 9 November 1825. He entered West Point in 1842 but had to be sent home during his junior year because of an illness contracted during the summer holiday. He re-entered the academy and graduated fifteenth in the class of 1847, beginning his service in the 1st Artillery and being promoted to second lieutenant. He fought in the Mexican War during 1847 and then in the Seminole War, but was detached from field duty and

employed as superintendent of the coast survey as a first lieutenant. Hill married Katherine 'Dolly' Morgan McClung on 18 July 1859, the sister of the future Confederate General John Hunt Morgan, and resigned his first lieutenancy in the US army in March of the following year in order to defend the honour of Virginia.

Hill entered the Confederate army as a colonel commanding the 13th Regiment Virginia Volunteers, but was commissioned brigadier-general by February 1862

and then major-general by 26 May of the same year, as a result of his distinction at the battle of Williamsburg (5 May 1862). During the remainder of 1862 Hill was involved in the battles of Mechanicsville, Chickahominy (June), Cold Harbor, Frayser's Farm and Richmond with his command, which had become termed 'the Light Division'. During the battles around Richmond (Seven Days) a disagreement emerged between Hill and his commander, James Longstreet, about an account of one of the battles.

As a result of this disagreement Hill was then ordered to join General Robert E. Lee in Fredericksburg (December), together with 'Stonewall' Jackson, his former classmate from West Point. They were involved against Banks at Cedar Run, against Pope at Second Bull Run (August), in the capture of Harper's Ferry (September) and against Burnside's forces at Sharpsburg, a battle which is reported to have been Hill's finest. Despite an ongoing quarrel with Jackson that eventually led to Hill's arrest, they then progressed to Chancellorsville (April 1863), where Hill assumed command of Jackson's corps after the death of his general.

Hill was also wounded by a shell in the back of his legs at this battle, but after recovering from his injuries, he was promoted to Lieutenant-General of the newly formed 3rd Corps on 24 May 1863 during the reorganisation of the Army of Northern Virginia. Hill's corps led the fighting in Gettysburg, although he became ill and had to follow his troops by ambulance on the second and third days of the battle, his men being turned over to other commands. As the result of errors in reconnaissance on the part of Hill during the battle of Bristoe Station (1863), the loss of men was enormous. Again, during the Wilderness Campaign in the spring of 1864, his illness made it impossible for him to lead his men from the front or to reorganise the lines, and he missed the battle of Spotsylvania because of hospitalisation.

Hill returned to the battlefield during the battles of North Anna and Cold Harbor, and his men held many of the main lines during the siege of Petersburg. General Robert E. Lee's aide, William Taylor, later wrote that 'The Petersburg Campaign was the diary of the command of A.P. Hill'.

On 2 April 1865, having returned from another bout of sickness, Hill rode out to attempt to rally his troops, but was shot through the heart, dying instantly, by a stray group of Union soldiers from the 6th Corps whose surrender Hill had demanded. It was reported that General Robert E. Lee's sad comments were made with tears in his eyes: 'He is at rest now and we that are left are the ones to suffer'. Hill's escort and staff charged the enemy and recovered his body, burying him at Petersburg without the usual military honours.

It is reported that 'Little Powell' Hill was a favourite amongst the men and officers of his command, but that he had often proved to be a rebellious and troublesome subordinate. General Robert E. Lee wrote of him, 'He fights his troops well and takes care of them', and further claimed that he considered Hill to be next to Jackson and Longstreet amongst his lieutenants.

In 1867 his remains were moved to Hollywood Cemetery, but again moved in July 1891 to a vault in the A.P. Hill monument; a statue, raised by the survivors of his famous Light Division, now stands over his grave in Richmond.

Hill, Daniel Harvey (1821–89)

Daniel Harvey Hill was born the youngest of eleven children in York District, South Carolina, on 12 July 1821. His grandfather, William Hill, a native of Ireland, had built Hill's Iron Works in York District and directed the casting of cannon for the Continental army until the works was eventually destroyed by the British. Hill's grandfather had fought as a colonel in Sumter's command.

Daniel Hill graduated from West Point in 1842, twenty-eighth out of fifty-six, along with Longstreet, A.P. Stewart, G.W. Smith, R.H. Anderson and Van Dorn, and entered the Maine Frontier. He soon rose to the rank of first lieutenant during the Mexican War, winning the brevet of captain at Contreras and Churubusco, and major at Chapultepec. During the Mexican War Hill fought in almost every battle under Scott or Taylor and gained recognition for his conspicuous courage. He resigned from the army at the end of this war and embarked on a teaching career in

mathematics at Washington College, Virginia, and then Davidson College, North Carolina. When war broke out he was Superintendent of the North Carolina Military Institute and the brother-in-law of 'Stonewall' Jackson, having married, in 1852, Isabella, the eldest daughter of Reverend Dr Robert Hall Morrison.

Following the battle of Big Bethel, Hill was promoted to brigadier-general, serving for a while in northern Virginia and leading a division at Yorktown, Williamsburg, Seven Pines and in the Seven Days battles, under the command of General Robert E. Lee, during the Peninsular Campaign, having further been promoted to major-general. He fought under Joseph E. Johnston at Yorktown, Williamsburg and Seven Pines, and for a short period of time he commanded the Department of North Carolina. At Williamsburg Hill's men were distinguished, and at Seven Pines Longstreet reported: 'The conduct of the attack was left entirely to Major-General Hill. The success of the affair is sufficient evidence of his ability, courage and skill.'

Hill remained in south-eastern Virginia during Second Bull Run but was called to rejoin Lee's army for the Maryland Campaign, where he and his troops performed well at South Mountain and Antietam.

It is reported that Hill was respected by his troops but that he was often harsh towards his fellow officers, even criticising his commanding officers in public. He was said to have criticised both Braxton Bragg and Robert E. Lee to such an extent that he received the condemnation of Jefferson Davis and the dislike of Robert E. Lee for the remainder of his life. Apparently Hill's criticisms of Lee came about as a result of the Confederate defeat at Malvern Hill and the loss of the famous 'Lee's lost order' (Special Order No. 191) containing the Antietam battle plan.

Despite this, Hill was promoted to lieutenant-general on 11 July 1863, being assigned to the Army of Tennessee under the command of Braxton Bragg and taking over the corps of Hardee. His defeat of Major-General William Rosecrans at the battle of Chickamauga brought him acclaim, but he attacked Bragg publicly for his failure to pursue the Union army and called for Bragg's removal from command.

It was Hill who was removed from command, and his promotion to lieutenant-general was withdrawn by Jefferson Davis on 15 October 1863. From this point onward during the war Hill held no other commands, seeing action briefly only at Petersburg (1864), when he served as a volunteer on Beauregard's staff at Drewry's Bluff and was in command of a provisional division for a few days, and Bentonville (1865). He finished the war with Joseph E. Johnston's army in the Carolinas as a divisional commander.

After the war Hill returned to teaching. He also became involved in editing two publications: a Charlotte magazine, *The Land We Love,* a Southern literature magazine which was published between 1865 and 1869, and *The Southern Home,* published between 1870 and 1877. When the publication work came to an end Hill continued to teach, and between 1877 and 1880 he was president of the Arkansas Industrial University and eventually president of the Military and Agricultural College of Georgia.

Daniel Harvey Hill died of stomach cancer at Charlotte, North Carolina on 24 September 1889, and was buried the following day in the then small college town of Davidson, about twenty miles north of Charlotte.

Hood, John Bell (1831–79)

(Library of Congress)

John Bell Hood was born the son of a doctor in Owingsville, Kentucky, on 29 June 1831. His uncle, Richard French, a member of the United States House of Representatives, managed to secure Hood nomination for a place at West Point. During his time at the Academy, Hood received several reprimands for his inappropriate appearance and behaviour, and for disobedience. At the time Robert E. Lee was the Superintendent of the Academy, and he charged Hood with the responsibility, as a lieutenant of cadets, to enforce stricter discipline. Within two months Lee had stripped Hood of this duty when he could make no explanation for his absence without authority. Whilst he was at West Point, George Thomas, the Union commander, taught Hood about artillery and cavalry tactics.

Hood graduated from West Point near to the bottom of his class in 1853, along with 45

McPherson and Schofield, serving two years in California as second lieutenant. The year 1855 found Hood serving under Albert Sidney Johnston and Robert E. Lee in frontier service in Texas, where he was wounded in 1856 at Devil's River. The following year he was promoted to first lieutenant, and at the outbreak of war he was serving as cavalry instructor at West Point.

On 16 April 1861 Hood resigned his commission and entered the service of the Confederate states, reporting to General Magruder on the peninsula of Virginia, as a brevet major. By September 1861 Hood had been promoted through the ranks to Colonel of the 4th Texas Regiment, and then brigadier-general in March 1862.

Hood was said to have led his troops daringly through the battles of Williamsburg and Seven Pines, and gained a reputation for hard fighting and reckless courage. His brigade was attached with the command of General Law at Eltham's Landing and Gaines's Mill, and it was reported by 'Stonewall' Jackson to have been 'the first to pierce the Federal entrenchments on the left and capture the batteries'.

He was further involved in the battles of Thoroughfare Gap, Gaines's Mill, Second Bull Run (August 1862) and the holding of Fox's Gap at South Mountain (September 1862) during the Maryland Campaign. During Second Bull Run Hood was arrested by General Nathan B. Evans after a dispute over some captured ambulances. Whilst under arrest he was permitted to accompany his division, and he was released by Robert E. Lee on the morning of the battle of South Mountain.

After fighting and distinguishing himself at Fredericksburg (December 1862), where he commanded the right of Longstreet's line, Hood led his division at Gettysburg (July 1863), where he was badly wounded in the arm by a shell fragment, whilst taking a leading role in Longstreet's attack against the Union left

at Little Round Top and Devil's Den. Hood was later breveted major-general, finally being promoted to the full rank the following October.

Hood rejoined from convalescence as Longstreet was moving west to join Bragg's command, and he took over command of the corps at Chickamauga (September 1863). He was wounded once more at Chickamauga, whilst distinguishing himself in the action by crushing the right centre of the enemy. This time the injury was to Hood's leg, which eventually had to be amputated, once more forcing him to retire and spend time recovering in Richmond.

On returning, Hood was given command of the corps on 18 July 1864, as a temporary general. His injuries, however, had left him so badly disabled that he had difficulty remaining on his horse. Hood made an ineffective attempt to take Sherman's army at Peach Tree Creek (July 1864), but managed to hold Sherman at bay at Atlanta. Jefferson Davis, aware that the Confederate army was being forced back to the outskirts of Atlanta, replaced Joe Johnston with Hood in command of the army. He began almost immediately to launch a series of attacks and counterattacks, but was unsuccessful in preventing Sherman from forcing him to evacuate Atlanta. Once he had fallen back, Hood unsuccessfully attempted to intercept Sherman's supply lines, and retreated to the Ohio Valley in the hope that Sherman would follow him. Instead Sherman sent George Thomas, Hood's previous tutor, to eventually force Hood to retreat from Nashville to Tupelo, Mississippi, where he relinquished his command in January 1865. Whilst Hood was travelling to Texas he was informed of the surrender of General Lee, surrendering himself on 31 May 1865.

Having settled in business in New Orleans at the end of the war, John Bell Hood, his wife and one of his daughters died of yellow fever on 30 August 1879, leaving behind him ten orphaned children.

Joseph Hooker was born in Hadley, Massachusetts, on 13 November 1814. He graduated from the class of 1837 at West Point, serving in the Seminole War and the Mexican War, but resigning from the army in 1855 as a result of an argument with General Winfield Scott. He then turned to farming in California, and after the battle of First Bull Run he failed to gain a commission in the Union army. Eventually, however, he received command of a brigade as a brigadier-general in August 1861, defending Washington.

After distinguished action at Williamsburg (April 1862) Hooker was promoted to major-general of volunteers and took part in the battles of Seven Pines and the Seven Days. He had gained the nickname 'Fighting Joe' by this time, and had gained a reputation as a heavy drinker and sometimes a disagreeable character.

By Second Bull Run (August 1862) Hooker had been transferred to Pope's command, but soon was given the command of a corps during the Maryland Campaign, where he was involved in the fighting at South Mountain and in the opening day of the battle of Antietam (September 1862), where he sustained a wound to his foot.

After the battle of Fredericksburg (November–December 1862) Hooker's commander, Ambrose Burnside, was relieved of his duty and Hooker was selected by President Abraham Lincoln to replace him as commander of the Army of the Potomac. In this role he entered the Wilderness Campaign, and after some confusion as to the intentions of General Robert E. Lee at Chancellorsville (April 1863), he was surprised by an attack by 'Stonewall' Jackson. Hooker had expected General Lee to withdraw, but Jackson's attack came very late at night. Jackson was killed, and Hooker also sustained a wound from an artillery shell at Chancellor House. On 3 May 1863 J.E.B. Stuart took over command of Jackson's troops and mounted another attack on Hooker's army. Stuart was reinforced the following day by Robert E. Lee and Jubal Early and by 6 May Hooker's army was forced to retreat across the Rappahannock river, having lost 11,000 men.

It is said that Lincoln lost confidence in Hooker after Chancellorsville, and although he remained in command of the army, he either resigned or was relieved early in the Gettysburg Campaign, on 28 June 1863, being replaced by General Meade. On 28 January 1864 Hooker received the Thanks of Congress for the beginnings of the Gettysburg Campaign, despite his criticisms of the control of the garrison at Harper's Ferry.

After the Union army was defeated at Chickamauga (September 1863) Hooker was sent to Chattanooga to reinforce the Army of the Cumberland with the 11th and 12th Corps. Here he was successful in

(Library of Congress)

taking Lookout Mountain and Missionary Ridge, and by the spring of 1865 the two corps had been merged into the new 20th Corps, with Hooker as their commander. In this role he fought through the Atlanta Campaign but asked to be relieved of his duties after McPherson had been killed and Oliver Howard received command of the Army of Tennessee. Claiming that he refused to serve under Howard, whom he considered to have been instrumental in his defeat at Chancellorsville, Hooker's request to be relieved of his duties was granted, and he spent the remainder of the war in Michigan, Ohio, Indiana and Illinois. He was finally mustered out as brevet major-general in the regular army for Chattanooga on 1 September 1866.

Two years later Hooker suffered a stroke and was forced to retire from the army with the rank of major-general on 15 October 1868.

Despite the fact that Hooker was said to have been popular with his men, he was often considered quarrelsome and insubordinate. It is also reported that, together with Dan Butterfield and Dan Sickles, Hooker was responsible for rounding up for his men the prostitutes that permanently followed the army, particularly in one area of Washington, when he was in command, hence the nickname 'hookers'. He is regarded by some to have been an immodest and immoral commander who frequently claimed slight by his superiors and often requested to be relieved of his duties.

Joseph Hooker died in Garden City, Long Island, New York, on 31 October 1879 and he is buried in Cincinnati.

Hopkins, Charles Fern (1842–1934)

Charles Fern Hopkins was born in Hope, Warren County, New Jersey, on 16 May 1842. His father was a harness maker, and Hopkins learned this trade from an early age, becoming renowned for the quality of his work, and eventually, in 1860, opening his own business in Boonton.

On 3 May 1861 Hopkins enlisted in the Union army and was mustered in at Trenton, New Jersey, on 4 June into Company I, First New Jersey Volunteers, under Kearny's New Jersey Brigade. Hopkins was involved in the battles of First Bull Run (July 1861), the Peninsular Campaign (May 1862) and Gaines's Mill (June 1862). During the fighting at Gaines's Mill Hopkins was wounded twice. But when he saw a fellow comrade, Sergeant Richard A. Donnelly, the late quartermaster-general of New Jersey, fall injured, Hopkins, despite his wounds, carried Donnelly across the battlefield to a place of relative safety. Whilst carrying out this heroic act, for which he was awarded the Medal of Honor, Hopkins was wounded for a third time, in the head, and both men were taken prisoner, Hopkins being reported dead.

After some time recovering from his wounds, Hopkins returned to his regiment during the Wilderness Campaign (1864) and was once more wounded and taken prisoner, spending the next ten months as a prisoner of war at Andersonville, Georgia, and Florence, South Carolina.

Hopkins was honourably discharged on 21 April 1865 at Trenton, New Jersey, and returned to his harness-making business. He married Hetty Ann Van Dyne on 8 January 1867, with whom he had nine children, and continued his life as a successful, prominent and well-respected member of the local community. In 1898 he was invited to erect a monument at Andersonville in commemoration of the New Jersey soldiers who had died there. In 1912, as president of the Kearny Commission, he had Philip Kearny's body exhumed from his unmarked grave and reburied with full military honours at Arlington National Cemetery, and in 1914 he erected a bronze equestrian statue above the grave.

In December 1927 Hopkins finally received his Congressional Medal of Honor, having never claimed it during the previous thirty-five years, through modesty. Charles Hopkins died on 14 February 1934 and was buried alongside his wife, who had died three years earlier.

Gaines's Mill, Virginia. (National Archive)

Oliver Otis Howard was born on 8 November 1830, the son of a farmer in Leeds, Maine. His father died when he was nine years old, and Howard attended a series of schools, finally graduating from Bowdoin College in 1850. Teaching for a while, he then secured a place at West Point through his Congressman uncle, in 1854, where he studied with W.D. Pender, S.H. Weed, Thomas H. Ruger, G.W. Custis Lee and J.E.B. Stuart. After graduating from West Point Howard went on to become an instructor in mathematics at the Academy between 1857 and 1861, married and became the father of three children. It is believed that, had war not broken out, then Howard would have been inclined to become a minister, as he had been studying theology and holding bible classes for enlisted men and civilians.

In June 1861 Howard resigned his commission in the regular army and enlisted as a colonel of the 3rd Maine. He commanded this brigade at First Bull Run (July 1861), being promoted to brigadier-general in September of the same year. Howard led his brigade at the battle of Seven Pines, where he received the Congressional Medal of Honor and promotion to major-general for his heroic actions on the battlefield. Whilst at the head of his brigade two horses were shot from under Howard and he sustained a serious injury to his right arm that resulted in its amputation.

When Howard returned from hospitalisation, he took part in the battles of Antietam (September 1862) and Fredericksburg (December 1862), where he commanded his division in what are considered by many to be the finest battles of his military career. Despite being disgruntled by the reorganisation of the army by Joseph Hooker, Howard continued as replacement for Franz Sigel as commander of the 11th Corps and led his troops to Chancellorsville

(April 1863). Apparently the German element of the 11th Corps was unhappy with the new appointment, and would have preferred Franz Sigel to remain in command. The morale of the corps was low and the German immigrants who had been recruited in the Middle Atlantic States were confused by Howard's distribution of bibles and their treatment from the remainder of the corps. When the corps was posted near the Wilderness Church, it is considered by many that they did not fight to their full potential. The result was a failure for the corps at Chancellorsville, and for Howard, who had embarked on his first battle as a corps commander.

In Gettysburg (July 1863) Howard experienced similar problems whilst attempting to take Oak Hill. But before Major-General von Steinwehr's division of Howard's corps could reach this defensive

(Library of Congress)

position it had already been taken by the Confederate army. Howard was forced to retreat to Cemetery Hill, where Major-General Hancock took command of the field, virtually ending Howard's involvement in the Army of the Potomac.

Howard was transferred to the west in command of the 4th Corps in the Atlanta Campaign and the Army of Tennessee in Sherman's march to the sea. He had received huge criticism for his involvements at Chancellorsville and Gettysburg, but was also considered to have been an active and considerate man, receiving the nickname 'The Christian Soldier', as well as a pious general and benefactor who had a strong moral conviction. After Chancellorsville Colonel Charles S. Wainwright, Chief of Artillery of the 1st Corps wrote of the criticisms of Howard: 'He is the only religious man of high rank that I know of in the army and, in the little intercourse I have had with him, shewed himself the most polished gentleman I have met.'

After the war Howard was appointed head of the Freedman's Bureau, and was active in supporting black suffrage, working to gain acceptance and equal rights for freed slaves. He founded an all-black college named the Howard University, and in 1872 assisted in securing peace with Native American tribes. As well as giving Howard a high profile, this also involved him once more in a great deal of controversy. He also served as Superintendent of West Point and wrote a number of biographies, including *Chief Joseph*, (1881), *Nez Percé Joseph*, (1881), *Zachary Taylor* (1892), his autobiography (1907) and *Famous Indian Chiefs I Have Known* (1908).

Oliver Howard died on 26 October 1909 in Burlington, Vermont.

The equestrian statue of Oliver Howard. (Lisa Mattson)

Jackson, Thomas Jonathan 'Stonewall' (1824–63)

Thomas Jonathan Jackson was born at Clarksburg, West Virginia, on 21 January 1824 to Jonathan and Julia (Beckwith Neale) Jackson. When he was two years old (March 1826), Thomas Jackson's father and elder sister, Elizabeth, died of typhoid fever, and the following day his mother gave birth to his youngest sister, Laura Ann. Having struggled with debts for several years, Jackson's mother remarried in 1830, but her new husband, Blake Woodson, disliked his stepchildren. The children were sent their separate ways, with Thomas Jackson and Laura now living with their relatives at Jackson's Mill, West Virginia and their brother, Warren, with their mother's family. Julia Jackson died in 1831 whilst giving birth to Thomas Jackson's half-brother, William Woodson, and Warren died of tuberculosis in 1841.

Thomas Jackson, having spent the remainder of his childhood with his uncles, entered West Point in 1842, graduating seventeenth out of fifty-nine on 30 June 1846. He entered the First Artillery Regiment as a brevet second lieutenant, serving in the Mexican War at Carlisle Barracks, Fort Hamilton and Fort Meade. He was commended during the war for his soldierly conduct and received promotions for his gallantry at Contrerar, Churubusco and Chapultepec, ending the war as a brevet major.

In 1851 Jackson resigned from the army to take up a teaching appointment at Virginia Military Institute (VMI), Lexington, and in 1853 he married Elinor Junkin, the daughter of the president of Washington College. Elinor and their stillborn child died on 22 October 1854. The year 1857 saw Jackson's second marriage, to Mary Anna Morrison, the daughter of the president of Davidson College. Their daughter, Mary Graham, was born on 30 April 1858 but died less than a month later. During 1859 Jackson, whilst serving at the VMI, was one of the academy's representatives who stood guard at the execution of the abolitionist John Brown.

Jackson was placed in command of the VMI cadets on 21 April 1861, and was ordered first to Richmond, where he was commander at Harper's Ferry. By June Jackson had been promoted to brigadier-general, and had gained the nickname 'Stonewall'. By October of the same year he had the rank of major-general in command of the Shenandoah Valley. During this battle General Barnard Bee, who was later killed on the battlefield, dubbed both Jackson and his command with the 'Stonewall' label. It was to remain with them both for the rest of the war and with Jackson throughout the future years, and having become a legendary figure, long after his death.

(Library of Congress)

This is the site of the Wilderness Tavern dependency. General Thomas Jackson had his arm amputated near here at the battle of Chancellorsville. (Malcolm Waddy III)

During the Shenandoah Valley Campaign (May–June 1862) Jackson won victories at the battles of Front Royal, Winchester, Cross Keys and Port Republic before being ordered, leaving reluctantly, to join General Robert E. Lee in eastern Virginia.

Following failures in the Seven Days battles (June–July 1862), Jackson tendered his resignation, but he was talked into withdrawing it and returned to the Shenandoah Valley. Between June and September he fought in the battles of Cedar Mountain, Clarke's Mountain, Second Bull Run and Antietam, and after Lee's reorganisation in October, he was promoted to lieutenant-general commanding the new 2nd Corps making up half of the Confede-

rate Army of Northern Virginia. Jackson then moved to Fredericksburg, where he spent the winter of 1862/3 before the battle of Chancellorsville (May 1863), having received news that his daughter, Julia, had been safely born in November 1862.

On 1 May 1863 the fighting at Chancellorsville opened, but the evening of the following day saw the accidental shooting of Jackson by a member of his own troops. He was shot in the left arm by three .57 calibre bullets and was taken to a hospital close to the battlefield, where his arm was amputated. Having been moved to a field hospital thirty miles away, he developed pneumonia, and died on 10 May. General Robert E. Lee, said to have been deeply emotional at the time of this accidental death, said of 'Stonewall' Jackson: 'He has lost his left arm; but I have lost my right arm.'

Thomas Jackson was buried on 15 May in Lexington, Virginia, where he had lived whilst teaching at the Virginia Military Institute. A monument was erected above his grave, reading:

The Stonewall Jackson monument is located near the Visitor Centre at Chancellorsville. (Malcolm Waddy III)

For centuries men will come to Lexington as a Mecca, and to this grave as a shrine, and wonderingly talk of this man and his mighty deeds. Time will only add to his great fame – his name will be honored and revered forever.

(Library of Congress)

Albert Sidney Johnston was born on 2 February 1803 in Washington, Kentucky, the son of John and Abigail (Harris) Johnston. He attended Transylvania University before entering West Point, from which he graduated as eighth in his class in 1826. He served at Sackett's Harbor, New York, in 1826, with the 6th Infantry at Jefferson Barracks, Missouri, in 1827 and as regimental adjutant in the Black Hawk War.

Johnston married Henrietta Preston on 20 January 1829, but because of an illness his wife had developed, he resigned his commission on 22 April 1834 in order to farm in St Louis. After Henrietta died on 12 August 1835, Johnston moved to Texas, and it is said that from this time onwards he considered himself to be a Texan. He enlisted as a private in the Texan army but was appointed adjutant-general in August 1836. By January 1837 Johnston had been wounded as a result of a duel fought with Felix Huston. Johnston had been lined up as a replacement for Huston as senior brigadier-general in command of the Texan army, but following his injuries he was unable to take up the post.

On 22 December 1838 Johnston was appointed Secretary of War for the Republic of Texas, and a year later he led an expedition against the Cherokee Indians in east Texas.

Johnston returned to Kentucky in March 1840 to marry Eliza Griffin, a cousin of his late wife, and the two returned to Texas, living at China Grove Plantation in Brazoria County.

As Colonel of the 1st Texas Rifle Volunteers, Johnston served as inspector-general at Monterey, Mexico, becoming paymaster in the US army and being assigned to the Texas frontier. He went to the Great Plains in 1855, and the following year was appointed Colonel of the 2nd Cavalry. During the following two years Johnston acted as brevet brigadier-general in the Salt Lake City expedition and was stationed at San Francisco in 1860.

In 1861 Johnston resigned his commission in the US army, refusing the Union army's offer of a command, and returned to Texas, where he was appointed a general in the Confederate army, commanding the western department, by an old friend of his, Jefferson Davis. This was one of the Confederacy's largest departments, and it extended from the Appalachian Mountains in the east to the Indian Territory in the west. Johnston had resigned his commission on 10 April but had refused to leave his post until his successor had arrived. Johnston joined the Confederate army with the reputation of being one of America's greatest living soldiers, and Jefferson Davis was said to have considered his services to be equal to a force of 10,000 men.

Johnston held his line of defence in Kentucky until it was broken at Mill Springs (January 1862) and at Forts Donelson and

54

Henry (February 1862). This was considered to have been one of his worst errors; dividing his field army had resulted in the loss of approximately 15,000 Confederate men, and criticism for this act continued for many years. Johnston then withdrew his command into northern Mississippi in order to regroup his men and prepare them for the battle of Shiloh (April 1862). He was very aware of the weaknesses of his army. They were lacking in organisation and small in number, and it was considered by many to have been a rash counter-attack on the part of Johnston.

At the battle of Shiloh, on 6 April 1862, Johnston was shot in the leg by a stray mini-ball whilst directing front-line operations in the area of the Peach Orchard, against Grant's army on the battlefield. He managed to force the Union army back, and was unaware of the severity of his wounds, so did not seek medical attention. Within a short time, however, he became weak and eventually bled to death on the battlefield. Shiloh had been Johnston's first and last great battle of the American Civil War, at the age of 59.

Albert Johnston, quoted as having been an imposing and noble-looking Southern aristocrat, was temporarily buried at New Orleans, but by special appropriation of the Texas government his remains were transferred to Austin in January 1867 and buried in the State Cemetery there. In 1905 a stone monument was erected above his grave.

CONFEDERATE

Johnston, Joseph Eggleston (1807–91)

Joseph Eggleston Johnston was born in Farmville, Virginia, on 3 February 1807. He entered West Point in 1825 and graduated in 1829 as thirteenth in a class of forty-six. He then spent eight years in the artillery before he was transferred in 1838 to the engineers and served in the Sac and Fox Wars, the Florida Indian Wars and the Mexican War, receiving commendation for distinctive service. Johnston won two brevets during the Mexican War and was wounded at Cerro Gordo and Chapultepec. He remained in the army, having been appointed quartermaster-general in June of 1860 until his resignation from the US army at the outbreak of the Civil War.

Johnston was initially commissioned into the Virginia forces as a brigadier-general, being promoted to full general on 31 August 1861. He was ordered to relieve 'Stonewall' Jackson at Harper's Ferry, in order to allow Jackson to move into the Shenandoah Valley, and continued Jackson's work in the organisation of the Army of the Shenandoah. After the Virginia forces were absorb-

ed into the Army of the Confederacy, Johnston's rank was reduced to that of brigadier-general. It was from Harper's Ferry that Johnston managed to trick the Union army into thinking that he had a large force, rather than the relatively small one he did have. This act allowed Johnston to move the bulk of his command to support Beauregard at First Bull Run by reinforcing from fresh troops who had arrived from the Shenandoah Valley.

Despite the glory of this success, Johnston was unhappy with his ranking. He considered that his previous experience and rank should have put him above that of Samuel Cooper, Albert Sidney Johnson and Robert E. Lee. As it stood at the time, Beauregard was the only commander who was placed below Johnston, and this would be the first of many conflicts between Johnston and Jefferson Davis. Some felt Johnston's considerations over rank and military etiquette to be petty ones that cost the Confederacy the opportunity of using his valuable services for lengthy periods of time.

55

Johnston appeared, however, to succeed in his 'petty complaints' and was promoted to the full rank of general; it was in this role that he was given command of the Department of Northern Virginia. He remained at Manassas during the winter of 1861/2, withdrawing when McClellan's Union army advanced. He then proceeded to reinforce John B. Magruder's troops on the peninsula east of Richmond, taking command of the area and again meeting McClellan at Yorktown (April–May 1862) and Williamsburg (May 1862).

In May 1862 Johnston launched an attack on McClellan's troops on the Chickahominy river, and fought at the battle of Seven Pines. He was wounded during this battle and replaced by General Robert E. Lee. After recuperating from his injuries Johnston returned to command the Department of the West, in charge of Bragg's Army of Tennessee and Pemberton's Department of Mississippi and East Louisiana.

Following the failures at Vicksburg (July 1863) and Chattanooga (November 1863), Johnston attempted to hold Jackson, Mississippi, against Sherman's army, and relieved Bragg's command. He succeeded in delaying Sherman's advance on Atlanta through the spring and summer of 1864, but his constant withdrawals brought criticism from Jefferson Davis, and he was relieved of his duties, with John B. Hood taking over his command. It was then considered that Hood's actions had become reckless, and the Confederate Congress called for Johnston to be reinstated. Despite some reluctance Jefferson Davis finally agreed to the reinstatement, and Johnston resumed command of the three departments early in 1865.

With a severe shortage of men, Johnston found it impossible to link up with the forces under the command of Robert E. Lee or to rally forces in the Carolinas. He eventually surrendered his forces on 26 April 1865 at Bennett House, near Durham Station, North Carolina.

After the war Johnston served in the House of Representatives and as Commissioner of Railroads. He wrote *Narrative of Military Operations*, which was published in 1874 and was critical of Jefferson Davis and many of Johnston's fellow generals.

Johnston attended the funeral of his wartime opponent, William T. Sherman, in New York City on 14 February 1891. Within a month Johnston had developed a serious cold as a result of attending Sherman's funeral, and he died on 21 March 1891. He was buried in Baltimore, Maryland.

(Library of Congress)

Philip Kearny was born in New York City on 1 June 1815, the only child of Philip and Susan (Watts) Kearny, a wealthy couple, and the nephew of Major-General Stephen Watts Kearny. Kearny's mother died shortly before his ninth birthday, and he appears to have found solace in solitary sketching of battle scenes and playing with his toy soldiers. After much family argument Kearny attended Columbia College, from which he graduated with an honours degree in law in 1833. After the death of his grandfather, who had been opposed to a military career for Philip, Kearny returned to New York, obtained a commission as a second lieutenant in the 1st US Dragoons and was sent to the French Cavalry School at Saumur. Whilst studying cavalry tactics here Kearny saw action in Algiers when he served with the Chasseurs d'Afrique. He returned to America and served as aide-de-camp to Alexander Macomb and Winfield Scott. In 1841 Kearny married Diana Moore Bullitt. After he was wounded at Churubusco during the Mexican War, the wound to his left arm resulted in its amputation, and Kearny was breveted major for gallantry. Partly as a result of this injury, combined with the insistence of his wife, Kearny resigned his commission. By 1859, however, he was serving in Napoleon III's Imperial Guard in the Italian War, where he won the French Légion d'honneur for bravery at Solferino. He had also divorced Diana.

When the Civil War broke out Kearny was appointed brigadier-general of volunteers and commanded a brigade of New Jersey regiments under the leadership of Brigadier-General William B. Franklin.

Kearny gave distinguished service during the Peninsular Campaign, and was promoted to major-general, commanding the 1st Division of Major-General Samuel P. Heitzelman's III Corps, on 4 July 1862.

Following the disaster for the Union army at Second Bull Run (August 1862), the battle of Chantilly was under way. During this indecisive battle Kearny rode into enemy lines during the darkness of the evening and was asked to surrender himself as a prisoner. Kearny refused and started to ride away, but was shot in the back and fell dead to the ground.

Philip Kearny was buried in Trinity Churchyard, New York City, but was later moved to the National Cemetery at Arlington, Virginia, and was buried with full military honours. In 1914 a bronze equestrian statue was placed above his grave and his New Jersey home town was later renamed 'Kearny'.

(Library of Congress)

Robert Edward Lee was born at Stratford, Virginia, on 19 January 1807, the son of General Henry Lee, also known as 'Light Horse Harry' of the American Revolution. His father died when Lee was eleven years old. Lee attended schools in Alexandria, being taught primarily by Mr William B. Leary, an Irishman, and he was prepared for his entrance to West Point in 1825 by Mr Benjamin Hallowell. It was said of Lee during his youth that he had a handsome face and a superb figure, coupled with a manner that charmed by cordiality, winning the respect of others by his dignity. It is not surprising then, that soon after graduating from West Point in 1829, without a demerit and with a second honours, Lee married.

The wedding, to Mary Custis, daughter of Washington Parke Custis, and granddaughter of Martha Washington, took place at Arlington, Virginia, on 30 June 1831. During this marriage Mary bore Lee seven children: G.W. Custis, Mary, W.H. Fitzhugh, Annie, Agnes, Robert and Mildred.

Lee entered military service as second lieutenant of engineers, and by 1834 had become assistant to the chief engineer at Washington, being promoted to first lieutenant in 1836 and captain of engineers in 1838. During 1837 he had, along with Lieutenant Meigs, been on the Mississippi river carrying out surveys and making plans for the improvement of navigation through the river. The year 1840 saw Lee a military engineer, stationed at Fort Hamilton, New York, and by 1844 he was also one of the board of visitors at West Point.

At the beginning of the Mexican War Lee was under the command of General Wool, but following a personal request from General Scott, he was assigned to the general's personal staff, effectively establishing batteries at Vera Cruz and Cerro Gordo. For his actions Lee was breveted major, and in his report Scott wrote of him: 'I am compelled to make special mention of Captain Robert E Lee.'

Among the officers with Lee in Mexico were Grant, Meade, McClellan, Hancock, Sedgwick, Hooker, Burnside, Thomas, McDowell, Albert Sidney Johnston, Beauregard, Thomas Jackson, Longstreet, Loring, Hunt, Magruder and Wilcox.

Lee also captured the attention of General Scott after his actions in the Valley of Mexico, when he wrote that Lee had performed: 'the greatest feat of physical and moral courage performed by any individual in my knowledge pending the campaign.'

Lee was further engaged in the battles of Contreras, Churubusco, Molino del Rey and Chapultepec, where he was wounded, and after which he was recommended for the rank of colonel.

When the Mexican War ended, Lee returned to Baltimore, and remained there until he served as Superintendent of West Point until 1855. He was then promoted to brevet lieutenant-colonel assigned to the 2nd Cavalry under the command of Colonel Albert Sidney Johnston, and serving alongside Hardee, Thomas, Van Dorn, Fitz Lee, Kirby Smith and Stoneman in the Frontier Wars.

Lee was in Washington during October 1859 when John Brown's raiding party was forced to surrender at his hands. He then returned to Texas until he was once again summoned to Washington, on 1 March 1861, by General Scott and asked to command the Union army. Francis P. Blair said to Lee at this meeting: 'I come to you on the part of President Lincoln to ask whether any inducement that he can offer will prevail on you to take command of the Union Army.' Lee replied: 'Although opposed to secession and deprecating war I will take no part in the invasion of the Southern States.'

Lee resigned his commission in the US army on 25 April 1861, becoming employed by the Confederate government the following month. He wrote to his sister, on 20 April 1861:

With all my devotion to the Union and the feeling of loyalty and duty of an American citizen, I have not been able to make up my mind to raise my hand against my relatives, my children, my home. I have therefore resigned my commission in the Army, and save in defense of my native State, with the sincere hope that my poor services may never be needed. I hope I may never be called on to draw my sword …

And again on 25 April:

No earthly act would give me so much pleasure as to restore peace to my country, but I fear it is now out of the power of man, and in God alone must be our trust. I think our policy should be purely on the defensive, to resist aggression and allow time to allay the passions and permit reason to resume her sway.

Jefferson Davis assigned Lee the command of the Department of Georgia, South Carolina and Florida, where he organised a system of coast defences. He was promoted to military advisor to the president the following March – a role in which he had some influence over military operations,

Harrison House was Robert E. Lee's headquarters during the first phase of the battle of Spotsylvania. (Malcolm Waddy III)

especially those of 'Stonewall' Jackson in the Shenandoah Valley.

During the battle of Seven Pines Joseph E. Johnston was severely wounded and Lee was instructed by Jefferson Davis to take over command of the reorganised Army of Northern Virginia. Leaving a small force at Richmond, Lee then entered the Seven Days battles on the other side of the Chickahominy river, fighting at Beaver Dam Creek, Gaines's Mill, Savage's Station, Glendale, White Oak Swamp and Malvern Hill. Although the battles ended in defeat for the Confederates, Lee had succeeded in preventing McClellan's army from threatening Richmond further.

Now considered to be a hero in the South, Lee acquired the nickname 'Uncle Robert', and moved on to a successful victory at Second Bull Run (August 1862). After the famous controversy concerning Special Order 191, when his orders for battle went missing, he was faced with fighting a delaying action against McClellan at South Mountain. However, after 'Stonewall' Jackson had successfully taken Harper's Ferry (September 1862) and rejoined Lee, they were successful at Antietam (September 1862) and were able to cross the Potomac river.

In the battles of Fredericksburg (December 1862) and Chancellorsville (April 1863) Lee was successful once more. But Gettysburg (July 1863) was a different story, and at Malvern Hill Lee made some of his first mistakes of the war, although they have been attributed to some of his subordinates.

Lee returned to Virginia after Gettysburg and commanded in the inconclusive battle of Bristoe Station (October 1863), and from the Wilderness (May–June 1864) he moved to Petersburg, where he fought a retiring campaign against Ulysses S. Grant. After finally being forced into a siege, Lee, becoming Commander-in-Chief of the Confederate Armies on 23 January 1865, managed to hold onto Richmond and Petersburg until April

1865, when he began his retreat to Appomattox. Gallantly trying to link up with Johnston, but unable to fight the troops under Grant and Sheridan's command, Lee stopped at Amelia to search for an escape route. He was attacked at Appomattox Station, with part of his army surrendering at Sayler's Creek on 6 April. Lee accepted Grant's terms of surrender on 9 April, finally surrendering at the Court House when resistance was no longer possible.

Lee returned to Richmond after the war as a paroled prisoner of war. Under the terms of the surrender he had been stripped of all rank and privileges, including his citizenship. But, writing on 5 January 1866, he urged his followers to forget the past and to 'make their sons Americans':

All that the South has ever desired was that the Union as established by our fathers should be preserved, and that the government as originally organized should be administered in purity and truth.

Declining many other offers, many of which would have ensured his family's financial security, Lee became president of Washington College (now the Washington and Lee University) in Lexington, Virginia. Lee's family home had been seized during the war by Union forces and is now a part of Arlington National Cemetery.

Robert E. Lee, who had become a legendary figure even before his death, died of a heart disease from which he had suffered since 1863. He finally passed away on 12 October 1870 in Lexington, Virginia, where he is buried. His application for the restoration of his citizenship had been mislaid, but eventually, in the 1970s, it was found and granted.

At a memorial service held in Lee's honour on 3 November 1870, Jefferson Davis said, 'He came from Mexico crowned with honors, covered with brevets, and recognized, young as he was, as one of the ablest of his country's soldiers.'

(Library of Congress)

James Longstreet was born in Edgefield District, South Carolina, on 8 January 1821. His father, also James, was a native of New Jersey, and his grandfather, William Longstreet, had been the first man to apply steam as power to a boat on the Savannah river, Augusta, in 1787. His maternal grandfather, Marshall Dent, was the first cousin of Chief Justice John Marshall. When James Longstreet was twelve years old his father died and he moved with his mother to north Alabama. It was from here that he entered West Point in 1838, graduating four years later with the brevet of second lieutenant stationed at Jefferson Barracks with the 4th Infantry. It was here that Longstreet met Ulysses S. Grant, whom he later introduced to his cousin, Julia Dent, the future wife of Grant.

In 1844 Longstreet joined the command of General Taylor in Louisiana, and the following year he was promoted to lieutenant of the 8th Regiment, based at St Augustine, Florida. Longstreet was involved in the battles of Palo Alto, Resaca de la Palma, Monterey, Vera Cruz, Cerro Gordo, San Antonio, Churubusco and Molino del Rey. By the time he reached the battle of Chapultepec he had been given the brevet ranks of captain and major, but following his wounding at this battle he was promoted through to major in 1858 until his resignation in 1861.

On 29 June 1861 Longstreet reported at Richmond, requesting an appointment in the pay department, but receiving a commission as brigadier-general reporting to Beauregard at Manassas. In command of the 1st, 11th and 17th Virginia regiments Longstreet was involved in the battle at Blackburn's Ford (July 1861), being promoted to major-general in October of the same year. In this role Longstreet commanded a division under Joseph E. Johnston at Yorktown, Williamsburg (May 1862), the battles of Seven Pines, and in command of his own plus the division of A.P. Hill, under Robert E. Lee, in the battles of Gaines's Mill and Frayser's Farm (June 1862) during the Seven Days. After the Union forces under McClellan retreated from Malvern Hill, Longstreet, in pursuit of McClellan at Harrison's Landing, commanded the 1st Corps of the Army of Northern Virginia, with 'Stonewall' Jackson leading the 2nd Corps. Longstreet followed Jackson into northern Virginia, where they jointly defeated Pope's Union army at Thoroughfare Gap. Longstreet then moved to hold the South Mountain passes, whilst Jackson's corps captured Harper's Ferry (September 1862).

After Sharpsburg (October 1862) Longstreet was promoted to lieutenant-general, becoming involved in the fighting at 61

Generals Lee and Longstreet consider the tactical options during the battle of Gettysburg. (Tim Hall)

Fredericksburg and the defence of Marye's Heights (December 1862). Moving for a brief time to Suffolk, Virginia, Longstreet then rejoined Lee at Fredericksburg after Jackson had been killed on the battlefield at Chancellorsville (April–May 1863).

Longstreet reached the battlefield on the first day of Gettysburg, and participated on the second and third days of fighting.

After Pickett's Charge on Cemetery Hill, Longstreet moved to reinforce Braxton Bragg in northern Georgia, commanding the left wing at Chickamauga (September 1863), then to Chattanooga (September–November 1863) and the capture of Knoxville (November 1863).

During the Wilderness Campaign (May–June 1864) Longstreet was seriously wounded, but having recovered sufficiently he rejoined his brigade at Richmond and Petersburg (October 1864), commanding the north side of the James river. Longstreet had gained the nickname 'Lee's Old War Horse', and he remained with Robert E. Lee until the surrender at Appomattox in April 1865.

After the war ended, Longstreet was told by President Johnson that he, along with Robert E. Lee and Jefferson Davis, would never receive amnesty. He became involved in business in New Orleans, and during the presidency of Ulysses S. Grant, whom Longstreet had befriended, he became a Republican and was appointed Surveyor of the Port of New Orleans, then Supervisor of Internal Revenue and Post-master. In 1880 he was appointed as the United States Minister to Turkey and then US Marshal for the District of Georgia, and finally, in 1897, the US Railroad Commissioner, succeeding the resigned General Wade Hampton, and serving under Presidents KcKinley and Roosevelt, from 1897 to 1904. Longstreet had been criticised by many former Confederates for his Republican activities, but his amnesty had been granted and he wrote, in retaliation, *From Manassas to Appomattox*.

James Longstreet died and was buried at Gainsville, Georgia, where he had settled after the war, on 2 January 1904, being the last of the high command of the Confederacy to die.

UNION
Lowe, Thaddeus Sobieski Constantine (1832–1913)

Thaddeus Lowe was born in New Hampshire in 1832 and became a renowned aeronautic scientist-inventor and one of America's first balloonists.

Shortly before the outbreak of war Lowe embarked on the first leg of a nine-hour, 900-mile transatlantic balloon flight from Cincinnati, Ohio. He was heading east in an attempt to prove that transatlantic navigation was possible. Having veered off course slightly because of strong, unexpected winds, Lowe landed on 20 April 1861 in the town then named Unionville, South Carolina. This was just a week after the fall of Fort Sumter, and the Confederate army arrested him on charges of spying for the Union army. Lowe managed to persuade the Confederates that he was innocent and was released from his imprisonment after only one day.

Lowe then returned to Washington, where he was appointed Chief of Army Aeronautics by Abraham Lincoln and commenced his intelligence-gathering work. He received the salary of a colonel and was allowed all the materials and labour that he required to carry out his espionage work.

Lowe's first information-gathering mission began shortly after First Bull Run (July 1861), and during the Peninsular Campaign (1861) he carried out reconnaissance flights on a daily basis, producing reports and photographs of the Confederate positions for George B. McClellan.

Lowe was given more money to increase the size of his fleet of gas-filled balloons, and eventually built seven airships. Each was manned by an observer and a telegraph operator, and these were used during the battles of Gaines's Mill (June 1862) and Chancellorsville (April–May 1863). The largest of the fleet was the *Intrepid*, which Lowe used for surveillance purposes during the battle of Fredericksburg (December 1862). It required 1,200 yards of silk and was 32,000 cubic feet in size. Several of the ships were shot down, and often failed in their missions because they were unable to return in time to provide the information to the command of the battles. As a result their use was abandoned in 1863 when Joseph Hooker was appointed commander of the Army of the Potomac.

Lowe continued his aeronautic development after the war in California, where the Lowe Observatory in Pasadena was built in memory of his war efforts and his scientific accomplishments.

Thaddeus Lowe's balloon gas generators, 1861. (National Archive)

UNION
McClellan, George Brinton (1826–85)

George Brinton McClellan was born on 3 December 1826 in Philadelphia, Pennsylvania. He attended the University of Pennsylvania before entering West Point. After graduating in 1846, second in his class, McClellan served with distinction as an engineer officer under Generals Zachary Taylor and Winfield Scott in the Mexican War. Through 1847 he was breveted first lieutenant and captain, finally being appointed as assistant instructor in practical military engineering at West Point from 1848 until 1851. The next four years saw McClellan as assistant engineer for the construction of Fort Delaware, and in the Marcy expedition.

He was promoted to chief engineer of the Department of Texas and then full captain in March 1855, being assigned to the new 1st Cavalry Regiment. He is famous for the development of the McClellan Saddle, which was adopted in 1856.

McClellan resigned from the army in 1857 to become a chief engineer and vice-president of the Illinois Central Railroad, becoming president of the Ohio and Mississippi Railroad in 1860. In May 1860 he married Ellen Nellie Marcy, the daughter of Captain Randolph B. Marcy, McClellan's commander during the western explorations.

On 23 April 1861 McClellan accepted a commission from Ohio's governor, William Dennison, as Major-General of the Ohio Volunteers, and was soon given command of the Department of Ohio in charge of all volunteers from Ohio, Indiana and Illinois. Shortly after First Bull Run (July 1861) McClellan crossed the Ohio river into western Virginia, preventing the Confederate forces from severing Washington's link with the west. It was after this initiative that McClellan gained the nickname 'Young Napoleon'.

It is said that McClellan actively worked for the retirement of the Commander-in-Chief of the Army, Winfield Scott, and lobbied to be promoted to the position. His efforts were rewarded when he was given command of the Army of the Potomac, but severe criticism has raged for years about his ability to put the army into battle. He was, apparently, a very organised commander who gained the loyalty and respect of his men, but was considered by many to have been over-cautious and the cause of too many delays.

After recovering from typhoid in December 1861, McClellan planned to advance on Richmond, commencing at Yorktown and then progressing to Williamsburg. Delays once again became too regular, and Abraham Lincoln suspended McClellan from command of all armies on 11 March 1862.

He was left to concentrate on the Army of the Potomac, and was successful in the two-day battle at the Seven Pines, but during the Seven Days (June–July 1862) McClellan's army was attacked by Robert E. Lee. Lee had amassed an army of 85,000 men and his counter-offensive actions led to the battles of Gaines's Mill, Savage's Station, Frayser's Farm and Malvern Hill. McClellan failed to take the advice of several of his officers to strike at Richmond, and ordered a change of direction from the York river to the James river, eventually settling at

Harrison's Landing. Lincoln then gave the order to abandon the campaign, and the majority of McClellan's forces were transferred to John Pope's army in northern Virginia.

After the defeat of Pope at Second Bull Run (August 1862), McClellan was restored to command the reformed army, leading his men to the battles of South Mountain and Antietam (September 1862), but he failed to stop Robert E. Lee once more, despite outnumbering the Confederates.

McClellan called for more men, equipment and fresh horses, but this did not assist him in his battle with J.E.B. Stuart, and he was once more ordered to relinquish command in November 1862. His inactive status was ordered by Abraham Lincoln for failure to pursue Lee after Antietam. Lincoln visited Antietam in an

George and Ellen McClellan. (Library of Congress) 65

attempt to urge McClellan to pursue Lee's army, and wrote:

I came back thinking he would move at once. But when I got home he began to argue why he ought not to move. I peremptorily ordered him to advance. It was nineteen days before he put a man over the river, nine days longer before he got his army across, and then he stopped again.

McClellan was ordered to return to his home in Trenton, New Jersey, and await new orders, which never arrived.

In 1864 McClellan stood against Lincoln as candidate for the presidency, and resigned from the army on election day. He then served as New Jersey's governor during the 1870s and 1880s. He died on 29 October 1885 at Orange, New Jersey and is buried in Riverview Cemetery, Trenton.

UNION
McDowell, Irvin (1818–85)

Irvin McDowell was born on 15 October 1818 in Columbus, Ohio. He was educated in France before entering West Point, from which he graduated in 1838, being posted to the artillery. McDowell became a tactics instructor at West Point, a post which he held until 1842, and then went on to serve on the staff of John E. Wood during the Mexican War. For his services at Buena Vista he was breveted major and worked as assistant adjutant-general from 1856 until the War of the States began.

Whilst serving in Washington McDowell was promoted to brigadier-general in the regular army and given command of the troops around the capital. At First Bull Run (July 1861) he was commanding troops who had little experience of conflict. He sent some of his troops to Blackburn's Ford along the Bull Run, but it was too much for them, and they failed to accomplish their mission. As a result of this, his first failure, McDowell was replaced by McClellan.

When the Army of the Potomac was reorganised McDowell was given command of the 1st Corps, the Department of the Rappahannock, with the responsibility of guarding the approaches to Washington. He was eventually meant to meet up with McClellan at the peninsula, but the Con-

federate army, under 'Stonewall' Jackson, in the Shenandoah Valley put a stop to this plan.

In the newly organised Army of Virginia, under the command of John Pope, McDowell was given command of a corps and was promoted to brevet major-general (in 1865) for his actions at Cedar Mountain (August 1862). Despite the fact that he was blamed for the Union failure at Second Bull Run (August 1862), a court of enquiry cleared him of any blame or

(Library of Congress)

accusation of misconduct. However, McDowell saw no further action during the war until he was made Commander of the Pacific Coast in 1864.

McDowell was mustered out of the volunteers on 1 September 1866, but continued to serve as a major-general in the regular army until he retired in 1882. He headed several war departments in the south and west, and later moved to California and was the Park Commissioner of San Francisco.

Irvin McDowell died on 4 May 1885 in San Francisco, California.

McLaws, Lafayette (1821–97)

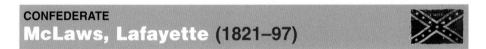

Lafayette McLaws was born on 15 January 1821 in Augusta, Georgia, and graduated from West Point in 1842. He served as a captain of infantry, fighting in the Mexican War, but resigned his commission in the Union army on 23 March 1861 in order to join the Confederate army.

McLaws organised the 10th Georgia Regiment as a colonel, being promoted to brigadier-general by September 1861. He then served in the Peninsular Campaign under Magruder and was involved in the battles of the Seven Days, being promoted to major-general in charge of his own division under Longstreet's command. During the Maryland Campaign he was involved in the battles of Harper's Ferry (September 1862) and Antietam (September 1862) and later at Fredericksburg (December 1862), Chancellorsville (April 1863) and Gettysburg (July 1863).

On the second day at Gettysburg McLaw's division was engaged in the Peach Orchard during the attack at Cemetery Ridge. After 'Stonewall' Jackson's death he was the senior major-general in the Army of Northern Virginia, and expected to take over command of the reorganised Army of Northern Virginia. Robert E. Lee, however, had concerns about McLaws's ability to command a corps, and chose A.P. Hill and Richard Ewell instead.

On 17 December 1863 McLaws was relieved of his command as a result of Longstreet's complaints about his assaults at Fort Sanders and Bean's Station. After a court of inquiry he was first of all ordered back to duty with his division, which was now stationed in Virginia. Eventually, however, he was sent to the southern coast, where he became involved in the battle of Bentonville in the defence of Savannah and served under J.E. Johnston during the rest of the Carolinas Campaign.

It has been said of McLaws that, although he proved himself to be capable, he was never considered brilliant enough to warrant any further advancement in the Confederate army.

After the war McLaws was involved in insurance, and also became a collector for the Internal Revenue and a postmaster. He died on 14 July 1897 in Savannah, Georgia.

(Library of Congress)

(Library of Congress)

Topographical Engineers and saw service at Palo Alto, Resaca de la Palma and Monterey in the Mexican War, receiving a brevet of first lieutenant. Meade's military engineering work involved him in the construction of lighthouses and breakwaters as well as in survey work.

On 31 August 1861 Meade was made brigadier-general of volunteers in command of a Pennsylvania brigade. After being stationed at the Washington defences, he then joined the Peninsular Campaign, fighting at the Seven Days (June 1862) in the battles of Mechanicsville, Gaines's Mill and Glendale. He was wounded twice at the battle of Glendale, but once he had recovered he went on to lead his brigade in Irvin McDowell's corps at Second Bull Run (August 1862) and at South Mountain (September 1862).

George Gordon Meade was born on 31 December 1815 in Cadiz, Spain, the son of a previously wealthy American merchant who had been financially ruined because of his allegiance to Spain during the Napoleonic Wars. Meade studied for some time at Mount Hope Institution in Baltimore before entering West Point in 1831. He graduated in 1835, nineteenth out of fifty-six, with little desire to remain in the army, and he resigned the following year to embark on a career in civil engineering. He re-enlisted on 19 May 1842 as a second lieutenant in the Corps of

At Sharpsburg Meade replaced John F. Reynolds, who had been sent to Harrisburg in order to enlist and train more troops, and commanded a division of Joseph Hooker's 1st Corps. By Fredericksburg (December 1862) Meade commanded the 3rd Division in Franklin's corps and then the 5th Corps at the battle of Chancellorsville (April–May 1863).

68 *The Meade pyramid, Fredericksburg. (Malcolm Waddy III)*

On 28 June 1863 Meade was given command of the Army of the Potomac. This command came about for a number of reasons. It was felt by the Union administration that Joseph Hooker should not command another battle. Another contender, Darius Couch, had been transferred, and John Sedgwick and Reynolds had agreed to serve under Meade.

During the Gettysburg Campaign (July 1863) Reynolds was killed in action, but the Army of the Potomac, under Meade's command, succeeded in repulsing the Confederate assaults, although they did sustain huge casualties. The Confederate army withdrew towards the Potomac river and in the middle of the month they managed to cross this.

The fact that the Confederate troops were allowed to cross the river provoked considerable criticism of Meade, who offered his resignation. This was declined, however, and Meade was promoted to brigadier-general in the regular army with effect from 3 July 1863 and was also awarded the Thanks of Congress on 28 January 1864.

During the remainder of 1863 Meade was involved in the battles of Bristoe Station and Mine Run, but by the spring of 1864 he had been joined by the restored Ambrose Burnside under the command of Ulysses S. Grant as Lieutenant-General and General-in-Chief. Although Meade was still nominally in command of the Army of the Potomac, Grant had chosen to make his headquarters with them, and so Meade reported directly to the commander. In this role he fought in the Wilderness Campaign (May–June 1864), at the battles of Spotsylvania (May), Cold Harbor (June) and then at Petersburg, and was rewarded with promotion to major-general. Meade continued with the Army of the Potomac until the surrender at Appomattox Court House in April 1865. When the hostilities terminated General Grant complimented Meade publicly, 'for the faithful manner in which he had performed the duties of his position'.

The Army of the Potomac had had five commanders, and Meade, the final one, had commanded it for half of its existence. In 1887, at the inauguration of a memorial in Meade's honour, Major-General John Gibbon said of Meade:

> *Of all the leaders who guided these heroes to final victory, this country produced no more courageous, more conscientious or more faithful in every trust committed to his charge than George Meade.*

After the war ended, George Meade was assigned to the command of departments and divisions in the east and south, and was in charge of the Military Division of the Atlantic, with its headquarters at Philadelphia. He died at Philadelphia on 6 November 1872 from pneumonia, and is buried in Laurel Hill Cemetery, Philadelphia.

Major-General George G. Meade equestrian monument.
(Lisa Mattson)

Meagher, Thomas Francis (1823–67)

Thomas Meagher was born in County Waterford, Ireland, on 23 August 1823, his father being a wealthy merchant and Member of Parliament. After graduating from Stoneyhurst College in England, Meagher became involved in the Irish Independence Movement and joined the Young Ireland Party in 1845. He was found guilty of treason in 1848 and sentenced to death, but the judgement was commuted to exile in Tasmania. After marrying there he fled the island in 1852 for New York, where he became an icon in the Irish-American community. His wife and son eventually joined him in America, and he went on to study law, opening a legal practice in 1855. In 1859 he defended Daniel Sickles for the murder of his wife's lover, and also became the editor of *Irish News*.

Joining the Union army in 1861, Meagher raised an Irish Zouave company, the 69th New York Volunteer Militia Regiment and served as a field officer at First Bull Run (July 1861). He was mustered out with his regiment in August of that year but went on to organise the Irish Brigade, which included several regiments from New York, Massachusetts and Pennsylvania.

The Irish Brigade was involved in the battles of the Peninsular Campaign and Second Bull Run (May 1862), and Meagher was promoted to Brigadier, leading the brigade at the battles of Seven Pines and during the Seven Days (June–July 1862). After an injury when his horse was wounded at Antietam (September 1862) and the slaughter of many of his men on Marye's Heights at Fredericksburg (December 1862), Meagher then fought at Chancellorsville (April–May 1863). He resigned when the War Department refused to replace the troops lost at the battle of Fredericksburg, and he became further embroiled in army politics. Meagher was a Democrat and highly critical of the Republican generals. His resignation was rejected, and he returned to duty in 1864 as a military administrator with the rank of brigadier-general, assisting at Savannah, Georgia, until he finally resigned on 15 May 1865.

After the war Meagher was appointed Secretary of the Montana Territory and served as acting governor of the state. On 1 July 1867 Thomas Meagher was accidentally killed when he fell off a steam boat on the Missouri river and drowned.

(Library of Congress)

70

John Morgan was born on 1 June 1825 in Huntsville, Alabama, moving to Kentucky at the age of six. After graduating from Transylvania University he enlisted in the army, seeing action during the Mexican War as a first lieutenant with the 1st Kentucky. After the war he married and settled in Lexington as a merchant, and in 1857 he organised the Lexington Rifles, a pro-Southern militia.

In 1861, despite the fact that Kentucky remained neutral, Morgan began smuggling rifles for the Confederates, and a warrant for his arrest was issued by the Union army. After the death of his wife, Becky, in July 1861, Morgan joined the Confederacy and led a squadron in central Kentucky and at the battle of Shiloh (April 1862) before being promoted to Colonel of the 2nd Kentucky Cavalry.

By October 1862 and the collapse of the Southern Campaign in Kentucky, Morgan had gained a reputation for his daring raids. In Murfreesboro (December 1862) he led a mounted division against Rosecrans's troops as a brigadier-general. He received the Thanks of Congress for his activities here, and he also met his future wife, Martha Ready.

In July 1863, during the Tullahoma Campaign, Morgan crossed the Ohio river against the instructions of his commander, Braxton Bragg, in what became known as 'Morgan's Great Raid'. He was captured in New Lisbon, Ohio, and imprisoned in the state penitentiary, escaping in November 1863 along with six of his men and returning to the south. Morgan was placed in command in east Tennessee and south-west Virginia the following year.

On September 4 1864 Morgan was staying at the home of a friend in Greeneville, Tennessee. His men were camped nearby, and a surprise attack by

(Library of Congress)

the Union army on Greeneville took them all by surprise. In an attempt to escape Morgan was shot in the back and killed by a Confederate-turned-Union private, Andrew J. Campbell.

John Morgan was buried in Richmond, Virginia, but on 17 April 1868 his remains, along with those of his brother, Tom, killed in 1863, were buried at Lexington Cemetery.

John Singleton Mosby was born on 6 December 1833 in Powhatan County, Virginia, to a wealthy family. He entered the University of Virginia but was expelled after he shot a fellow student, George Turpin, in the jaw. He was imprisoned in Charlottesville Prison but eventually released after the efforts of his family and friends gained him a pardon. Mosby then studied law and opened his own small legal practice, and married Pauline Clark, the daughter of a former Kentucky Congressman, on 30 December 1857.

In 1861 Mosby enlisted as a private in the 1st Virginia Cavalry, but after some disagreements with the unit's colonel, he was transferred as a scout to the troops of J.E.B. Stuart. He became involved in the Peninsular Campaign (May 1862), and after being imprisoned for a short time, he was given permission to raise a band of partisans for service in the Loudoun Valley, northern Virginia.

'Mosby's Raiders', as his men had become known, succeeded in forcing Union field commanders to deploy large numbers of troops to guard their supplies and communication lines. Mosby often carried out the advance scouting himself under disguise.

During 1863 Mosby, together with twenty-nine of his partisan raiders, caused havoc to the Union army, but not without a great deal of criticism from many of the Confederate supporters. They captured General Edwin Stoughton at Fairfax Court House, and after Generals Crook and Kelley were taken prisoner by another band of raiders, Mosby complimented them, saying he could only surpass their success by capturing Abraham Lincoln himself. Many commanders took to executing the raiders rather than continue with the disruption they were causing.

Mosby refused to surrender in 1865, but preferred to disband his command. He was finally pardoned the following year and returned to his law practice, but lost the little respect he had gained from Southerners when he befriended Ulysses S. Grant, a Republican. Mosby became a US Consul in Hong Kong, and finally died in Washington on 30 May 1916. He is buried in Warrenton Cemetery.

(Library of Congress)

72

Pelham, John (1838–63)

John Pelham was born in Benton County (now Calhoun County), Alabama, on 7 September 1838, the son of a doctor, remaining in the state until he joined West Point in 1856. He was still a student here, having embarked on the only five-year course the Academy ever offered, when war broke out in 1861.

He returned to Alabama and was commissioned as first lieutenant of artillery in the regular Confederate States army based in Lynchburg, Virginia. He was then assigned as drillmaster to Alburtus's Battery at Winchester and became involved in the battle of First Bull Run (July 1861). He impressed his commander, General J.E.B. Stuart with his gun-handling skills, and was entrusted by him with the organisation of a unit of horse artillery.

In this role Pelham's artillery fought in the battles of Williamsburg (May 1862), Cold Harbor, Second Bull Run (August 1862), Sharpsburg, Shepherdstown and Fredericksburg (December 1862). After his gallant and courageous efforts at Fredericksburg, General Robert E. Lee said of Pelham, referring to him from then on as 'the Gallant Pelham', 'It is glorious to see such courage in one so young'.

Bull Run, where John Pelham impressed J.E.B. Stuart. (National Archive)

73

Pelham was promoted for his bravery at Fredericksburg, but his commission did not reach him in time. Having heard of a proposed action at Kelly's Ford (17 March 1863) Pelham joined the unit involved, despite the fact that he was not even attached to it. He was hit in the head by a shell fragment and presumed dead. It was not until he arrived at the field hospital on the back of a horse some hours later that he was found to still be alive.

Because of a lack of prompt attention he finally died shortly after his arrival at the hospital.

John Pelham's body was laid in state in the Confederate Capitol Building in Richmond, Virginia, as a tribute to his bravery. After eventually being returned to Alabama, he was buried, after lying in state once more, in the Jacksonville City Cemetery in Calhoun County. He was twenty-four years old when he died.

CONFEDERATE
Pickett, George Edward (1825–75)

George Edward Pickett was born into a prosperous 'old' Virginian family of plantation owners in Richmond on 25 January 1825, and was the cousin of Henry Heth. After studying law in Illinois he received his appointment to West Point through the office of Congressman John Stuart. Pickett studied for the four years at West Point, together with his classmates George B. McClellan and Thomas J. Jackson, graduating last in his class in 1846. He was 25 when he married his sweetheart, Sally Minge, who was also a Richmond, Virginia, native. But Pickett's marriage was short-lived, his wife dying after only eleven months of marriage.

During the Mexican War Pickett was breveted lieutenant and captain for his activities in the siege of Vera Cruz and the advance on Mexico City. At Chapultepec, when Lieutenant James Longstreet was wounded he handed the regimental colours to Pickett, who carried the flag up and over the wall. The two men continued to serve together throughout the remainder of the war, and when it ended Pickett was stationed in temporary command of Company K at Fort Bliss, Texas. In 1854 his relief was sent; it was Longstreet, and Pickett remained second-in-command to him until 1855, when he was transferred to Washington Territory, remaining there until 25 June 1861, when he resigned his commission to join the Confederate army.

He was appointed a colonel in the Confederate army on 23 July 1861, and served on the Rappahannock river in the Department of Fredericksburg and the Aquia District, Department of Northern Virginia.

On 14 January 1862 Pickett was promoted to brigadier-general in command of a brigade in Longstreet's division under General Joseph E. Johnston. In this role he fought during the Seven Days Campaign (June–July 1862), being wounded at the battle of Gaines's Mill (27 June). His shoulder wound prevented his involvement in further action until October of the same year, when he was promoted to major-general in command of a division in the Army of Northern Virginia at the recommendation of his close friend Longstreet.

After the battle of Fredericksburg (December 1862) Pickett served in Longstreet's Tidewater Campaign in southeastern Virginia. July 1863 saw Pickett at the battle of Gettysburg, where his name in the history of the war was secured with his failed 'Pickett's Charge', ordered by Robert E. Lee on the third day (3 July). Longstreet was given the responsibility of planning and ordering an assault on the Union centre. Pickett commanded the brigades of Kemper, Garnett and Armistead, and the forward movement began in mid-afternoon. Pickett

(Library of Congress)

unsuccessfully attempted to co-ordinate the movement, finally being forced to withdraw his troops when the task became impossible and after a huge loss of men.

Shortly after the battle of Gettysburg, Pickett married again, this time LaSalle Corbell, with whom he had two sons, George Jr and Corbell.

In September 1863 Pickett was sent to North Carolina in command of the Department of North Carolina, where he gave distinguished service at Drewry's Bluff, rejoining the Army of Northern Virginia at Cold Harbor (June 1864). Pickett also served at New Bern and in the Petersburg Campaign (1865), being involved in the battles of Dunwiddie Court House and Five Forks (April 1865), where his division was virtually destroyed. Robert E. Lee relieved Pickett of his command at Sayler's Creek a few days before the surrender, but he surrendered with the army at Appomattox Court House on 9 April.

After the war had ended, Pickett fled to Canada. He had been prosecuted for alleged actions against Union prisoners from North Carolina at New Bern. He was eventually pardoned by General Grant and returned to America, but was said to have suffered from severe depression, and brooded on the loss of his division at Gettysburg for the rest of his life. Refusing to accept offers of commands from Egypt and the United States, he settled in Norfolk, Virginia, where he worked in the insurance business as a salesman in Richmond. He was said to have been a dapper man, with shoulder-length hair worn in long, perfumed ringlets. He died on 30 July 1875, and his body was placed in a temporary vault until October of the same year, when his remains were transported to his native Richmond, where he was buried at Hollywood Cemetery with full military honours.

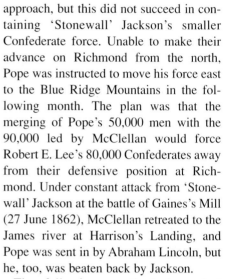

John Pope was born in Louisville, Kentucky, on 16 March 1822. He graduated from West Point in 1842 and was assigned to the topographical engineers. He performed with credibility, being considered by many to be a good soldier, and was engaged in Florida, and in the survey of the north-east boundary between America and Canada. During the Mexican War Pope served under General Zachary Taylor and participated in the battles of Monterey and Buena Vista, being breveted through the ranks of first lieutenant and captain. After the Mexican War he remained in the army, being variously employed in the carrying out of surveys on the Pacific Railroad and on lighthouse duty.

As a captain Pope served in the escort of Abraham Lincoln to the Washington inaugural ceremony, and was appointed brigadier-general of volunteers the same year. He performed organisational duties in Illinois before serving under Fremont in the western department, where he had some success in Missouri and was given a command in the Mississippi Campaign. During this campaign Pope was successful at New Madrid and Island No. 10, and in the advance on Memphis, as well as at Corinth, where he led one of the three armies under the command of Henry Halleck.

On 26 June 1862 Pope was promoted to major-general in command of the newly formed Army of Virginia, with the responsibility of protecting Washington and controlling the Shenandoah Valley. His former commander, Fremont, refused to serve in Pope's corps and was relieved of his duties. It was not a popular command amongst the troops either, as Pope had lost the faith of his men by making an address that praised the western armies and criticised the efforts of the eastern forces. Pope was said to have had an aggressive

approach, but this did not succeed in containing 'Stonewall' Jackson's smaller Confederate force. Unable to make their advance on Richmond from the north, Pope was instructed to move his force east to the Blue Ridge Mountains in the following month. The plan was that the merging of Pope's 50,000 men with the 90,000 led by McClellan would force Robert E. Lee's 80,000 Confederates away from their defensive position at Richmond. Under constant attack from 'Stonewall' Jackson at the battle of Gaines's Mill (27 June 1862), McClellan retreated to the James river at Harrison's Landing, and Pope was sent in by Abraham Lincoln, but he, too, was beaten back by Jackson.

The following month Jackson had moved to protect the town of Gordonsville, which was sited at a railroad junction between Richmond and the Shenandoah Valley. Pope ordered Nathaniel Banks to assault Gordonsville, but he was defeated at the battle of Cedar Run (9 August) and Pope called for McClellan to rejoin the battle for the railroad junction, but after

(Library of Congress)

Lee reinforced his numbers with all the men available to him, their attempts again failed.

At the battle of Second Bull Run (August 1862) Pope was blamed for the Union defeat. Pope had been attacked by Jackson and Longstreet and been forced to retreat across the Bull Run. The Army of Virginia had been pursued by the Confederate army until they had reached Chantilly on 1 September. Some 15,000 men had been lost in this three-day battle, and it was later claimed of Pope that 'he was entirely deceived and outgeneralled. His own conceit and pride of opinion led him into these mistakes.'

After he blamed the defeat at Second Bull Run on his subordinates, Pope came into conflict with several supporters of McClellan and was relieved of his command and sent to Minnesota. The Army of Virginia was merged into the Army of the Potomac a few days later, with McClellan given its command, despite reservations about this placing by Abraham Lincoln.

Pope spent the remainder of the war years ably commanding the Department of the North-west and dealing with the Sioux uprising, for which he was breveted major-general in the regular army in 1865. He was mustered out of the volunteers on 1 September 1866. From 1870 until 1883 he was commander of the Department of the Missouri, with the responsibility of protecting settlers from Native American attacks. He had been given the full rank of major-general in October 1882 and retired from the army in 1886. John Pope died in Sandusky, Ohio, on 23 September 1892.

UNION
Reynolds, John Fulton (1820–63)

John Fulton Reynolds was born in Lancaster, Pennsylvania, on 21 September 1820 to Lydia and John Reynolds. He graduated twenty-sixth out of fifty-two in 1841 and entered the regular army, serving in the Mexican War and receiving two brevet promotions for gallantry and meritorious conduct. He was also involved in the Utah expedition before being appointed commandant of cadets and instructor of tactics at West Point in 1860.

On 14 May 1861 Reynolds was promoted to lieutenant-colonel and assigned to the 14th US Infantry, but by August of the same year he had been promoted to brigadier-general of volunteers. He was assigned to the command of a brigade of the Pennsylvania Reserves, responsible for training in the Washington area. He then served as military governor of Fredericksburg and took command of a brigade in the Army of the Potomac in June 1862.

He was involved in the battle of Beaver Dam Creek (26 June) during the Seven

Side view of the equestrian statue of John F. Reynolds. (Lisa Mattson)

Days (June–July 1862). After the battle of Gaines's Mill (27 June) Reynolds was captured, but he was exchanged on 13 August of the same year and commanded the Pennsylvania Rangers at Second Bull Run (August 1862) and during the Maryland Campaign.

On 29 November 1862 Reynolds was promoted to major-general, and commanded the 1st Corps of the Army of the Potomac

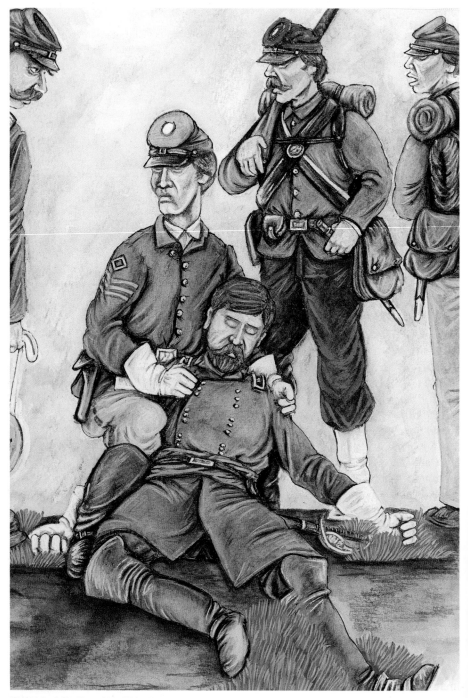

The death of John Reynolds at Gettysburg. (Tim Hall)

at Fredericksburg (December 1862) and Chancellorsville (April–May 1863). After Chancellorsville Reynolds became disenchanted with the leadership of Joseph Hooker, and reported his feelings to Abraham Lincoln in Washington. As a result Meade, rather than Hooker, was given command of the army and Reynolds led the 3rd Corps to Gettysburg (July 1863).

On the first day of the battle, whilst personally directing the deployment of his 'Iron Brigade', Reynolds died as the result of being hit by a rifle bullet. His death, on 1 July 1863, was considered to be the loss of one of the Union's greatest generals, who was trusted and respected by his men and his superiors. His troops had bestowed him with the nickname 'Old Common Sense', and Joseph Hooker had called him 'one of his ablest officers'. John Reynolds was buried at Lancaster Cemetery, Pennsylvania.

Rosecrans, William Starke (1819–98)

William Rosecrans was born on 6 September 1819 in Kingston, Ohio, to Crandell and Jane (Hopkins) Rosecrans, originally from Holland. His great-grandfather had signed the Declaration of Independence as governor of Rhode Island and had co-authored the draft Articles of Confederation. Rosecrans graduated, fifth in his class, from West Point in 1842, along with his fellow students James Longstreet, Richard Anderson, Arthur Doubleday, John Newton, George Sykes, Seth Williams, Lafayette McLaws, Alexander P. Stewart, John Pope, D.H. Hill and Earl Van Dorn. He had shared quarters at the Academy with Longstreet and Stewart. After serving in the engineer corps, Rosecrans returned to West Point as a professor, remaining in post until 1847, when he resigned to take up work as an architect and civil engineer. He became president of a navigation company, and in 1857 he organised the Preston Coal Oil Company in Cincinnati, Ohio. He also became known for his inventions, the experiments for which caused him to be so badly burned that he was incapacitated for more than a year.

When civil war broke out Rosecrans enlisted in the state of Ohio, and became drillmaster for the 'Marion Rifles', then engineering officer in charge of the Camp Dennison project, and eventually commanding officer of the 23rd Ohio Volunteer Infantry.

He was promoted to brigadier-general in the regular army, commanding his troops against Robert E. Lee at Rich Mountain, Virginia (11 July 1861). When Fremont was placed above him and McClellan failed to give him any credit for his actions at Rich Mountain, Rosecrans requested a transfer to the west, where he was sent to the command of Halleck. He was then given command of two divisions of the Army of the Mississippi, taking part in the battles of Iuka, against Price, and Corinth, against Price and Van Dorn. After Corinth some disagreements with Ulysses S. Grant developed, and Rosecrans accepted the offer of command of the Army of the Cumberland on 24 October 1862.

At Murfreesboro (December 1862) Rosecrans faced Braxton Bragg, and despite the fact that the battle was indecisive, he received the Thanks of the Nation for his actions. He then began planning the Tullahoma Campaign, and when the War Department complained that he was taking too much time, he moved to Chattanooga, where he failed to consolidate, resulting in the battle of Chickamauga (September 1863), once again against Braxton Bragg. Rosecrans was driven back to Chattanooga, and General George H. Thomas was left on Snodgrass Hill faced with 60,000 Confederate soldiers. Thomas managed to retreat and was not pursued, and the Union army had regained control 79

of Chattanooga, but Rosecrans had been defeated. It is reported that Rosecrans had been demoralised by his defeat but that he did contribute strongly to the plans for the next battle of Chattanooga (23–25 November) when the Union army was successful. However, despite this success, Rosecrans was replaced by George Thomas in command of the Army of the Cumberland, an act which virtually ended his involvement in the future campaigns of the war.

Rosecrans was given command of the Department of the Missouri, where he remained until the surrender in 1865. Despite his non-involvement, however, it is said that he remained popular with the public and those who had served under his command.

After almost accepting the nomination for the Republican candidacy for Vice-President in 1864, he served in minor capacities until he resigned from the army in 1867 in order to resume his career in business. He moved to Los Angeles, California, and became an advocate for railroad building in the west and Mexican trade. In 1868 he was appointed Minister to Mexico, a post which he held for the next two years. In 1870 he began developing mines in Nevada, the south-west, and Mexico, continuing this work for the remainder of the decade. Between 1881 and 1885 he served in the US House of Representatives as the Californian Democratic Representative and became chairman of the Committee on Military Affairs. He was then appointed to the US Treasury and was restored to the rank and pay of a brigadier-general of the regular army on the retired list.

Rosecrans retired to a ranch in Los Angeles in 1893, remaining there until 1898 when he died on 11 March in Redondo, California. He is buried in Arlington National Cemetery.

Safford, Mary Jane (1834–91)

Mary Jane Safford was born on 31 December 1834 in Hyde Park, Vermont, but moved with her family when she was three years old to Crete, Illinois. When her parents died in 1849, Safford was brought back to Vermont, where she lived with family and attended the Bakersfield Academy. She then took up a position as governess to a German family in Canada, learning French and German, and on return to America she lived with her brother, Alfred Safford, in Joliet, Shawneetown, and by 1858 in Cairo, Illinois.

When war broke out Cairo became strategically important for the Union army because of its situation at the meeting of the Ohio and Mississippi rivers. Because the town became occupied by large numbers of volunteers, the hastily constructed camps soon became prone to epidemic diseases, and Safford began her nursing career.

She tended the sick as best she could and prepared and distributed food. When 'Mother' Mary Ann Bickerdyke arrived during the summer of 1861, Safford answered her appeal for volunteer nurses in the military hospitals that had been constructed. They tended the sick in the camps and the wounded from the battles. At the battle of Belmont, Missouri, Safford, searching out the wounded on the battlefield, carried aloft her own flag of truce. After the battle of Fort Donelson (February 1862) Safford was exhausted, having transported the wounded to Cairo. Mary Bickerdyke reported later that Safford had worked without sleep for ten consecutive days. Despite her exhaustion Safford then volunteered for nursing duties on the *City of Memphis*, but this proved to be too much and she returned to her brother's home.

She returned in April 1862 for the battle of Shiloh, and nursed on the *Hazel Dell*, a transport boat, where her compassion towards the wounded won her the name 'Angel of Cairo'. However, exhausted once more, she was forced to recuperate at her home, after which time she embarked on a European tour and did not return to America until the war had ended.

In 1867 Safford entered the New York Medical College for Women, graduating two years later to take up advanced training in Europe for a further three years. She returned to America in 1872, having married James Blake, and opened a private practice in Chicago the following year. She became professor of women's diseases at the Boston University School of Medicine and a staff physician at the Massachusetts Homeopathic Hospital. Poor health forced her to retire in 1886, and she moved to Tarpon Springs, Florida, where she died on 8 December 1891.

'Mother' Bickerdyke, mentor to Mary Safford. (Library of Congress)

Winfield Scott was born in Petersburg, Virginia, on 13 June 1786, to a wealthy and famous American family. He attended the College of William and Mary in Williamsburg, Virginia, and entered his military career. As lieutenant-colonel he fought during the War of 1812, being captured on 11 October during the battle of Queenston Heights, and wounded at the battle of Lundy's Lane. He returned to military duty to fight in the Indian Wars (1832), commanding the Union army during the Trail of Tears, and in the Mexican War (1846–8) he commanded the US forces. Scott was an unsuccessful Whig presidential candidate in 1852, and by this time had gained the nickname 'Old Fuss and Feathers' because of his pedantic assertion to protocol.

By the time the Civil War erupted, Scott had been America's General-in-Chief for twenty years and was approaching seventy-five years of age. Because of his large stature, weighing 300 lb and being 6 ft 5 in tall, he had begun to suffer from gout and vertigo and was unable to ride a horse. He requested the appointment of a field officer and suggested to Abraham Lincoln that Robert E. Lee be offered the post. Lee turned it down because of the implications of having to fight the state of his birth, and the job was given to George McClellan.

(Library of Congress)

Scott then developed his 'Anaconda Plan', recommending naval blockades to squeeze the Confederate army, and despite initial criticism this plan eventually proved effective when used by Abraham Lincoln.

On 1 November 1861, after the battle of Ball's Bluff, a Union defeat, Scott offered his resignation, and this was accepted by Abraham Lincoln. His successor was George McClellan, and Scott retired to write his memoirs and travel.

The following year the idea of the Medal of Honor was strongly criticised by Scott, who felt it inappropriate to adopt the European custom of awarding medals for heroism.

Scott lived the remainder of the war as an observer. He watched virtually all the elements of his Anaconda Plan being used, and saw the Confederate army defeated. Winfield Scott died on 19 May 1866 at West Point, New York, where he is buried despite the fact that he never attended the Academy.

John Sedgwick was born on 13 September 1813 in Cornwall Hollow, Connecticut. He attended Sharon Academy and then embarked on a short teaching career until entering West Point, from which he graduated in 1837 as twenty-fourth in his class, along with Joseph Hooker and Jubal Early. After being post-ed to the artillery, Sedgwick fought in the Seminole War, the Indian Wars and the Mexican War. In 1855 he was transferred to the cavalry and served as major on the Mormon expedition, having received two brevets during the Mexican War.

Sedgwick was promoted to lieutenant-colonel in March 1861, and twice replaced

This monument marks the approximate location of where Major-General John Sedgwick was killed by Confederate sharp-shooters during the battle of Spotsylvania. (Malcolm Waddy III)

Robert E. Lee during the first months of the war. He took over command of General Charles P. Scone's division when this officer was placed under arrest, and led his troops to the peninsula. He was involved in the battles of Yorktown and Seven Pines, being wounded at Frayser's Farm (1862). Having been promoted to major-general on 4 July 1862, he led his division at Antietam (September 1862), where he was wounded three times and forced to recuperate, missing the battle of Fredericksburg.

When he returned, he was variously given command of three divisions – the 2nd, 9th and then the 6th. He commanded the largest corps of Joseph Hooker's force at Chancellorsville (April–May 1863), and in an attempt to storm the position held by Jubal Early at Marye's Heights was forced to withdraw from Salem Church and fall back to a hurriedly constructed pontoon bridge. His corps then moved to Gettysburg (July 1863), where they were held in reserve close to the Rappahannock river. After the reorganisation of the Army of the Potomac, Sedgwick retained his command, leading his men to the Wilderness (May–June 1864).

At the battle of Spotsylvania (8–14 May) Sedgwick, who had become affectionately known as 'Uncle John' by his men and recognised for his common sense and courage, was shot in the head by a Confederate sharpshooter on the Brock Road, and died immediately. John Sedgwick was the last Army of the Potomac corps commander to be killed in action on the battlefield, and was buried in his home town of Cornwall Hollow, Connecticut.

Shaw, Robert Gould (1837–63)

Robert Gould Shaw was born the only son of the relatively wealthy abolitionist family of Francis George and Sarah Blake (Sturgis) Shaw on 10 October 1837 in Boston, Massachusetts. From the age of three to nine years Shaw lived with his family in an experimental commune near Brook Farm. They then moved to the East Coast, and for some time lived in Europe, where Shaw attended a boarding school in Switzerland and travelled extensively. In 1856 he entered Harvard University, and after graduating worked for some time in his uncle's business in New York. In 1860 he enlisted with the 7th New York National Guard, but by 10 May 1861 he was serving as a captain in the 2nd Massachusetts, a newly formed company.

During the Shenandoah Valley Campaign Shaw's regiment was ordered to cover the retreat from Strasburg, and in the battle of Front Royal (23 May 1862) he received a minor wound. The 2nd then

(Library of Congress)

Shaw leading the 54th Massachusetts. (Library of Congress)

moved to Cedar Mountain (9 August) where they sustained enormous casualties, and on to Antietam (17 September) where Shaw suffered another minor wound.

Following Abraham Lincoln's Emancipation Proclamation of 1 January 1863, Shaw was approached by Governor John A. Andrew to form a black volunteer regiment from freed slaves, the 54th Massachusetts, and lead it as their colonel. The regiment was mustered into service on 13 May 1863 and sent to Charleston, South Carolina. Shaw led the regiment in battles on James Island, Legaresville (13 July) and Secessionville (16 July), and then the troops marched through the mud flats to Morris Island. Shaw and the 54th had proved themselves fully capable of standing up to the enemy fire.

On 18 July Shaw, having confidence in the ability of the 54th, accepted the challenge offered by General Strong to lead the charge to attack Fort Wagner. That evening he led his men along the beach to the fort, rallying them to scale the walls of the fort. The losses were enormous, and as Shaw reached the top of the parapet he was struck by a bullet and killed.

In an attempt to insult Shaw, some of the rebels, who had been against the arming of black soldiers, buried him in a common grave with his enlisted freedmen. When his family heard of this act they stated their pleasure in that they felt this would have been what their son would have wanted.

85

Joseph Orville Shelby was born on 12 December 1830 in Lexington, to one of Kentucky's wealthiest families. He attended Transylvania University, and after graduating became engaged in rope manufacturing until 1852. He then moved to Waverley, Missouri, to a career in steamboating and hemp growing.

In the spring of 1861 Shelby entered the Missouri State Guard as a captain of a ranger company, and fought at the battles of Carthage, Wilson's Creek and Pea Ridge (1861–2).

Shelby was then ordered back to Missouri to form a regiment, and was promoted to Colonel of the 5th Mississippi Cavalry. Commanding a brigade, the 1st Corps, in John S. Marmaduke's cavalry division, Trans-Mississippi Department, he became involved in the battles at Prairie Grove (7 December 1862) and Helena (4 July 1863), where he was wounded and had to retire from the battlefield in order to recuperate.

When Shelby returned, he was promoted to brigadier-general in the Confederate

The Rio Grande where Joseph Shelby plunged his 'stars and bars' rather than surrender the flag to the Union. (National Archive)

States army, and led a brigade at the battle of Jenkins' Ferry (30 April 1864). Remaining with the Trans-Mississippi Department, Shelby then led a cavalry division during Price's invasion of Missouri (September–October 1864), remaining in this role until the Confederate surrender of April 1865.

When Robert E. Lee surrendered at Appomattox Court House, Shelby, along with other Confederates, refused to surrender, but chose instead to march some of his force to Mexico. They left their camp at Corsicana, Texas, passing through Waco, Houston, Austin and San Antonio. In June 1865 he sank his divisional battle flag into the Rio Grande river rather than have to surrender it to the Union army. En route they had enforced martial law and killed guerrillas and bandits. It was Shelby's intention to offer the services of his brigade to Emperor Maximilian, but once they arrived he discovered that his march had been futile and that many of his men preferred to return home.

Shelby then returned to his business interests in Missouri, and farmed and harvested wheat in Lexington. He also became involved in the promotion of railroads and the operation of coal mines. In 1893 he was appointed US Marshal, a position he held until he died, on 13 February 1897.

UNION
Sheridan, Philip Henry (1831–88)

(Library of Congress)

Although the exact date of his birth is not certain, Philip Henry Sheridan was probably born to his Irish immigrant parents on 6 March 1831 in Albany, New York. After spending his childhood years in Somerset, Ohio, Sheridan entered West Point in 1848 by appointment of Congressman Thomas Ritchie, who was a friend of the family. It took him five years to graduate because of a disagreement with a fellow student, the future Union army General William R. Terrill. Sheridan had been suspended for a year after threatening Terrill with a sword and fighting with him when he had reported the incident to the authorities at the Academy. After graduating thirty-fourth of fifty-two in his class in July 1853 he joined the 1st Infantry as a second lieutenant at Fort Duncan, Texas. He was transferred to the 4th Infantry in the Pacific North-west in 1855, and the following year was promoted to first lieutenant assigned to the Grand Ronde Indian Reservation in Yamhill County, Oregon.

The outbreak of the Civil War found Sheridan promoted to captain, and in September 1861 he was ordered to St Louis under the command of General Halleck. He served in a staff position for the first year of the war, but at the request of General Gordon Granger he was given command of the 2nd Michigan Cavalry

Located five miles behind the Union lines, the Old Church Hotel served as headquarters for Major-General Philip H. Sheridan at Cold Harbor. (Malcolm Waddy III)

and promoted to colonel (25 May 1862). In this role he was successful against the Confederate General Chalmers at Booneville, Mississippi (July 1862), when he tricked the Confederates into thinking his force of 800 men had been reinforced. Because of his actions at this battle Sheridan was promoted to brigadier-general and ordered to the town of Rienzi, Mississippi, and then on to the battles of Perryville (October 1862) and Murfreesboro (December 1862).

He was promoted to major-general in April 1863, and arrived at the Viniard Farm at dusk on the evening of the first day of the battle of Chickamauga (19 September 1863). His division, along with almost two-thirds of the Union army, was swept from the field at this battle, resulting in the court martial of some of the other commanders. However, the battle of Chattanooga (September–November 1863) was more of a success for Sheridan and the Union army. His actions and those of his troops brought the Union victory after they participated in the charge of Missionary Ridge and broke through the Confederate lines.

Ulysses S. Grant was impressed with the aggressive actions of Sheridan, and when Grant was appointed General-in-Chief of the Union armies on 12 March 1864 he promoted him to Chief of Cavalry of the Army of the Potomac. In this role

Sheridan led the raid on Richmond (May 1864) during the Overland Campaign against J.E.B. Stuart, who was killed in action at Yellow Tavern.

From August 1864 to February 1865 Sheridan, as commander of the Army of the Shenandoah, was involved in driving the Confederate troops under the command of Early from the valley. He fought in the battles of 3rd Winchester (19 September 1864), Fisher's Hill (22 September) and Cedar Creek (19 October). It was whilst rallying his troops after the battle of Cedar Creek that Sheridan made his famous 'ride' from Winchester. He received the Thanks of Congress and was named brigadier and major-general in the regular army.

In March 1865 Sheridan destroyed the Confederate forces still remaining under the command of Jubal Early at Waynesboro before progressing to Lynchburg. Together with Grant, whom Sheridan had rejoined, they fought at the battle of Five Forks (1 April), and then, commanding a combined force of infantry and cavalry, Sheridan led the Union advance to Appomattox, where he was present at the surrender of Robert E. Lee.

After the war Sheridan remained in the army, heading the reconstruction government of Texas and Louisiana as military governor. He then organised campaigns against the Plains Indians, commanded the Division of the Missouri and observed the Franco-Prussian War. He worked for the creation of the Yellowstone National Park and in 1884 replaced William Sherman as Commander-in-Chief of the Army. He was presented with the elevated grade of full general by Congress and began writing his *Personal Memoirs*.

It is reported that Abraham Lincoln once said of Sheridan, who was 5 ft 5 in tall, 'He is a brown, chunky little chap, with a long body, short legs, not neck enough to hang him, and such long arms that if his ankles itch he can scratch them without stooping.'

Philip Sheridan died of heart disease on 5 August 1888, and he is buried in Arlington National Cemetery.

UNION
Sherman, William Tecumseh (1820–91)

William Sherman was born in Lancaster, Ohio, on 8 February 1820. His father died when he was nine years old, and his mother, unable to cope with the family, sent Sherman to be fostered by Thomas Ewing, whose daughter, Ellen, he later married. His brother, Thomas, had been sent to be cared for by an aunt. After being educated at West Point and graduating sixth in his class in 1840, Sherman was posted to San Francisco during the Mexican War. He received a brevet for his services in California, and when he resigned in 1853 in order to become a partner in a bank, he had been breveted a captain and commissary officer. He then became Superintendent of the Louisiana State Seminary and Military Academy at Alexandria, Louisiana. On 18 January 1861 Sherman resigned his position, and the following month he left Louisiana, returning to Ohio, where he remained until March, when he moved his family to St Louis, Missouri, and was elected president of the Fifth Street Railroad.

On 20 June 1861 Sherman accepted the rank of colonel in the 13th Regular Infantry, assuming command of a brigade in the 1st Division of McDowell's army under Brigadier-General Daniel Tyler. In this role he was involved in the First Bull Run (July 1861).

In August 1861, at the request of General Robert Anderson, Sherman was

From September to November 1863, having been given command of the Army of Tennessee, Sherman fought in the battle of Chattanooga, unsuccessfully assaulting the Confederate troops at Missionary Ridge under the command of Patrick Cleburne, but forcing the troops to retreat into Georgia. For his efforts he was made overall commander of the armies in the west and was given the Thanks of Congress.

Sherman's Atlanta Campaign began in May 1864, and after the battle of Kennesaw Mountain (27 June), where he was defeated by Joseph Johnston's Confederate troops, he finally entered Atlanta on 2 September 1864. Sherman declared the city a military encampment, and the civilians living there were forced to leave. He then began planning his 'March to the Sea'.

In November 1864 Sherman, having left Atlanta a blazing inferno, began marching to Savannah, setting fire to anything he felt could be of use to the Confederate forces over the sixty miles. He reached and occupied Savannah on 23 December and sent a telegram to Abraham Lincoln, informing him that he was presenting the President with Savannah as a Christmas present. He then began his march through South Carolina, fighting against Johnston's troops at the inconclusive battle of Bentonville (March 1865) and accepting the surrender of Johnston at Raleigh, North Carolina, on 17 April 1865.

Sherman received a second Thanks of Congress for his operations in Atlanta and Savannah, becoming the only man to twice receive it. He remained in the army after the war and was promoted to full general, replacing Ulysses S. Grant as Commander-in-Chief when the latter took up presidential office. After establishing the Command School at Fort Leavenworth, Sherman retired from the army on 8 February 1884 and made his home in New York, where he died on 14 February 1891. He is buried in Calvary Cemetery, St Louis.

transferred to the Department of the Cumberland and promoted to brigadier-general. By October of the same year he had relieved Anderson as commander of the Department of Kentucky, but only held this post until he was replaced by Don Carlos Buell, when he was sent to the Department of the West in St Louis, Missouri, under the command of Major-General Halleck. He had requested this transfer after criticism of his actions in east Tennessee that led to the hanging of many Unionist partisans.

On 13 February 1862 Sherman relieved Ulysses S. Grant in command of the post at Paducah, Kentucky. After the reorganisation of the Army of Tennessee the following month, Sherman was placed in command of the 5th division of the army.

At the battle of Shiloh (April 1862) Sherman led his division of the Army of Tennessee, and once they had been reinforced by Buell's forces, they were successful in forcing the Confederate army to retreat, although Sherman had been wounded. In July of the same year Sherman was assigned to command the District of Memphis and made a failed attempt to take the Confederate stronghold of Vicksburg at Chickasaw Bluff.

Sickles, Daniel Edgar (1819–1914)

Daniel Edgar Sickles was born in New York City on 20 October 1819. He attended New York University, and after studying law decided to make politics his career, becoming the Corporate Consul of the City in 1847. He resigned the same year to become Secretary of the US Legation in London, and served from 1857 to 1861 as New York State Senator and Representative in Congress. He became the first man to be acquitted of a murder charge on the grounds of temporary insanity. On discovering that his wife had been having an affair with Francis Key, the son of Francis Scott Key, the author of *The Star-Spangled Banner*, Sickles shot the man dead in Lafayette Square in 1859.

At the outbreak of war Sickles, serving as a Democrat in the War Office, was appointed brigadier-general of volunteers on 1 September 1861, assigned to command the New York Excelsior Brigade. He commanded this brigade at Seven Pines and during the battles of the Seven Days (June–July 1862), and was in charge of the division at Fredericksburg (December 1862). He had been promoted to major-general the previous month.

When Joseph Hooker took command of the army, many complaints were made about the army headquarters, said to have been turned into a brothel, with claims that Sickles and Daniel Butterfield had assisted Hooker in this conversion.

After Hooker was removed after the battles at Chancellorsville (April–May 1863), Sickles retained command of the 3rd Corps and led his men in the battle of Gettysburg (July 1863). His troops had been located along Cemetery Ridge, near Round Tops, but Sickles, who disliked this location, decided to advance on Peach Orchard, where he was overrun by Longstreet's assault. His 3rd Corps was

(Library of Congress)

virtually wiped out and his command was terminated by a serious wound to his right leg. His leg had to be amputated, and he donated it to the Army Medical Museum in Washington. He also received the Medal of Honor for his (now considered controversial) decisions.

Sickles was assigned a series of special missions by the War Department and made Colonel of the 42nd Infantry in 1866, being mustered out of the volunteer service as a major-general at the start of 1868. He retired in 1869 and was appointed US Minister to Spain. After serving for a term in Congress, he chaired the New York State Monuments Commission, being removed from this position in 1912 on the accusation of misuse of funds. He died on 3 May 1914 in New York City, and is buried in Section 2 of Arlington National Cemetery.

Edmund Kirby Smith was born on 16 May 1824 to his lawyer and judge father in St Augustine, Florida. After a West Point education he graduated in 1845 and served in the Mexican War under Generals Zachary Taylor and Winfield Scott, being breveted for gallantry. When the war ended he taught mathematics at West Point and served in the cavalry of the frontier. He also had botany reports published by the Smithsonian Institution.

In 1861 Smith resigned from the Union army and enlisted in the Confederate army, serving as Joseph E. Johnston's head of staff in the Shenandoah Valley, reaching the rank of brigadier-general by June 1861. In this role he commanded the 4th Brigade of the Army of the Shenandoah, fighting at First Bull Run (July 1861) and being so severely wounded that he had to spend time recovering. He returned to the battlefield as a major-general and division commander in northern Virginia.

Smith then moved, along with Braxton Bragg, into Kentucky, reaching Covington by September 1862 and fighting at the battles of Perryville (October 1862) and Murfreesboro (December 1862). After his success at Richmond, Smith was promoted to the newly created grade of lieutenant-general.

In February 1863 Smith was given command of the Trans-Mississippi Department. When Grant captured Vicksburg in July 1863, giving the Union army control of the Mississippi river, Smith had become isolated from the rest of the Confederate forces and saw little action for the remainder of the war. He did, however, defeat Nathaniel Banks in the Red River Campaign during the spring of 1864, and sent forces to reinforce against Steele in Arkansas.

(Library of Congress)

By the end of the war Smith had been promoted to a full general, and he was the last commander to formally surrender his forces, at Galveston, Texas, on 2 June 1865.

After the war he considered living in Mexico, but abandoned this idea when he was elected president of the University of Nashville, serving from 1870 until 1875. He then taught mathematics at the University of the South, Sewanee, Tennessee, from 1875 until 1893, where he died on 28 March 1893, being the last surviving full general of either army.

'JEB' Stuart was born in Patrick County, Virginia on 6 February 1833 to an 'old' American family, being the youngest son of ten children. He was the son of Archibald Stuart, a lawyer and soldier of the 1812 War and representative in the Virginian legislatures and conventions. Stuart studied at Emory and Henry College and entered West Point, graduating in 1854 thirteenth in his class, being commissioned a second lieutenant in October of that year and serving in Texas during the Indian Wars. He had gained a reputation for being a hard charger who never gave in. He was transferred to the new 1st Cavalry in May 1855, based at Fort Leavenworth. On 14 November 1855 he married the daughter of Colonel Philip St George Cooke at Fort Riley, and by the turn of the year he had been promoted to first lieutenant. During 1857 he fought in the battle of Solomon's River, where he

was wounded. He accompanied Robert E. Lee in 1859 on his mission to end John Brown's seizure of the Harper's Ferry arsenal. Stuart went forward and read the note calling on Brown and his followers to surrender, and signalled for the assault which recaptured the building when the terms of surrender were refused.

He was promoted to captain in April 1861, but resigned his commission with the Union army in order to join the Confederacy.

On 10 May 1861 Stuart was commissioned lieutenant-colonel of Virginia Infantry and ordered to Harper's Ferry to join 'Stonewall' Jackson, being promoted to colonel within two months. After this early service in the Shenandoah Valley, Stuart led his men in the battle of First Bull Run (July 1861). Jubal Early wrote of Stuart after First Bull Run: 'Stuart did as much toward saving the battle of First Manassas as any subordinate who participated in it.'

Stuart was promoted to brigadier-general on 24 September 1861, being transferred to the Peninsula to fight at the battles of Yorktown (April–May 1862) and Williamsburg (May 1862). He was again promoted, on 25 July 1862, to major-general for his services at Richmond.

During the Seven Days (June–July 1862), Stuart would ride the battlefield dressed in his famous black-plumed hat, caught up with a gold star, and flowing cloak. He gained prominence throughout the South after his famous ride around McClellan's Army of the Potomac during the Peninsular Campaign. Although the raid caused little real damage, it embarrassed McClellan and confirmed to Robert E. Lee that the Union commander's right flank was poorly guarded. Stuart's report, which was published afterwards in the Richmond newspapers, made him a hero to the Southern cause. He continued serving gallantly and thoroughly through the Seven Days Campaign, confirming McClellan's move to Harrison's Landing. He was to become one of Robert E. Lee's most famous and popular subordinates.

After the battle of Second Bull Run (August 1862), during which Stuart lost his hat whilst in pursuit of Union troops during one of his raids, he managed to capture vital documents, which enabled Robert E. Lee to gather information about the Union's intentions.

After the battles of Antietam (September 1862) and Fredericksburg (December 1862), Stuart took over the command of his friend 'Stonewall' Jackson's corps after the general was killed during the battle of Chancellorsville (April–May 1863). Before Jackson died he sent this message to Stuart: 'Tell General Stuart to act on his own judgement and do what he thinks best. I have implicit confidence in him.'

Stuart then fought at the inconclusive battle of Brandy Station (9 June 1863), but in the three-day battle of Gettysburg (July 1863) Stuart arrived during the second day, having been marching for eight days and nights, and became involved in the fighting of the third day. He was defeated in his attempt to attack the Union right, but managed to stop the Confederate supply trains from falling into Union hands at Williamsport whilst retreating.

During the campaign in the Wilderness (May–June 1864) Stuart succeeded in halting the Union cavalry at Yellow Tavern, close to Richmond, but in the battle he was wounded and transported to a hospital in Richmond. He died there the following day, 12 May 1864, as a result of his injuries and was buried in Hollywood Cemetery.

General Fitz Lee said at the Veterans Banquet on 28 October 1875 of the wounded Stuart: 'His voice – I can even now hear – after the fatal shot was fired, as he called out to me as I rode up to him, "Go ahead, Fitz, old fellow, I know you will do what is right", and constitutes my most precious legacy.'

(Library of Congress)

of the volunteers involved in this, the first major battle of the war.

Sykes was first given command of a brigade of regulars in March 1862, leading them in the battle of Yorktown (April–May), and then the 2nd Division, 5th Corps, made up of predominantly regular soldiers. This division became known as 'Sykes's Regulars' and they became involved in the fighting at Gaines's Mill (27 June), where Sykes was commended.

At the Second Bull Run (August 1862) Sykes's Regulars were involved in the fighting withdrawal of John Pope's command. They were then in reserve at Antietam (September 1862), and in November of the same year Sykes was promoted to major-general, being involved in the battles at Fredericksburg (December 1862).

At the start of the battle at Chancellorsville (April–May 1863) Sykes's command led the Union army's flanking movement towards the rear of Robert E. Lee's troops, but was counter-attacked and ordered to retreat by Joseph Hooker. Having proved himself an effective defensive commander, Sykes had not, however, excelled in attack.

When George Meade was promoted just before the battle of Gettysburg (July 1863), Sykes was given his command of the 5th Corps of the Army of the Potomac, becoming involved in the fighting on the third day of the battle. This command was short-lived, however, and he was removed from his position after the battle of Bristoe Station and Mine Run (October 1863).

George Sykes was born in Dover, Delaware, on 9 October 1822. He graduated from West Point, where he had roomed with D.H. Hill in 1842, thirty-ninth out of fifty-six. During his infantry service in the Seminole and Mexican Wars, during which he was breveted, and in his time at West Point, he had gained the nickname 'Tardy George'.

Sykes commanded the only regular army infantry to take part in First Bull Run (July 1861), and was promoted to brigadier-general in September 1861. It was felt that his regular soldiers were paramount in controlling the over-enthusiasm

Sykes spent the remainder of the war years in Kansas, and was mustered out of the volunteers at the beginning of 1866. He died on active duty as a colonel of the 20th Infantry at Fort Brown, Texas, on 8 February 1880.

(Library of Congress)

George Thomas was born in Southampton County, Virginia, on 31 July 1816, and lived on his family's farm until they were forced to flee to the city during the Nat Turner revolt. He entered West Point in 1836, sharing a room with William T. Sherman, and graduated twelfth in his class in 1840. He was commissioned second lieutenant in the 3rd Regiment of Artillery, being promoted to first lieutenant after the Seminole War. He received two brevets for his services in the Mexican War, and went on to teach artillery tactics at West Point in 1851. He married Frances Lucretia Kellogg the following year, and was promoted to major in 1855, being wounded in 1860 on the Texas frontier.

Despite being disowned by members of his family, Thomas remained with the Union army at the outbreak of war. He was promoted to colonel in command of the 2nd US Cavalry (later the 5th), leading his troops in the Shenandoah Valley, but by August 1861 he had been promoted to brigadier-general of volunteers in the Department of the Cumberland.

He fought at the battle of Mill Springs (January 1863), was promoted to major-general of US volunteers, then commander of the 14th Corps, Army of the Cumberland, after the battle of Murfreesboro (January). Thomas then organised the Union's defences at Chickamauga (September 1863), where he gained the nickname 'The Rock of Chickamauga', after which he succeeded Rosecrans in command of the Army of the Cumberland. In this role he was paramount in the Union victory at Chattanooga (November 1863), which led to the subsequent capture of Atlanta (September 1864).

Now a brigadier-general in the regular army, Thomas moved to Nashville (December 1864) and then directed the forces that captured Selma, Alabama (April 1865), receiving the Thanks of Congress and promotion to major-general in the regular army as a result of his heroic actions.

After being involved in the pursuit and capture of Jefferson Davis on 10 May 1865, Thomas remained in the army. He was said to have been the most effective military governor of Kentucky, Tennessee, Mississippi, Alabama and Georgia, and in 1869 he accepted command of the Division of the Pacific, based in San Francisco. After suffering a stroke whilst working at his headquarters in San Francisco, Thomas died at the age of fifty-four on 28 March 1870.

Tompkins, Sally Louisa (1833–1916)

Sally Louisa Tompkins was born on 9 November 1833 in Poplar Grove, Mathews City, Virginia. By the time the Civil War broke out in 1861, however, she was living in Richmond, having moved there with her mother after the death of her father.

After the battle of First Bull Run (July 1861), the Confederate government appealed for assistance from the public in the treatment of those who had been wounded on the battlefield. Tompkins, who had a substantial inheritance, opened a private hospital, the Robertson Hospital, in a house donated by Judge John Robertson for the purpose.

She successfully and efficiently cared for the wounded. As more soldiers who had been treated by her were subsequently returned to fight again, the officers made every attempt to place their wounded men in the Robertson Hospital, rather than other alternatives.

On 9 September 1861 Tompkins was appointed as an unassigned captain of cavalry in order to adhere to the government regulation that ordered all hospitals to be run by military personnel. In this rank, with the nickname 'Captain Sally', she was the only woman to have held a commission in the Confederate army. Tompkins was paid an officer's salary, and this enabled her to subsidise the huge costs involved in running the hospital. Several other hospitals in the Richmond area were being shut down, but Tompkins persuaded Jefferson Davis to allow hers to remain open because of its high success rate in recovery.

Richmond, Virginia in April 1865, as Sally Tompkins would have seen the Confederate capital. (National Archive)

The hospital remained in existence until June 1865, with a record of only 73 deaths out of the 1,333 Confederate soldiers who had been treated there.

Tompkins, whose inheritance had been exhausted by her activities, became active in the Church after the war and was often invited as a speaker at reunions and meetings of the Daughters of the Confederacy.

Virtually penniless, she lived in the Confederate Women's Home, Richmond from 1905 until her death on 26 July 1916.

She was given a full military funeral and made an honorary member of Robert E. Lee's Camp of the Confederate Veterans. The United Daughters of the Confederacy named four of their branches in her honour.

UNION
Harriet Tubman (1820–1913)

Although Harriet Tubman's exact date of birth is not known, it is believed that she was born during either 1820 or 1821, but it is definitely known that she was born into slavery in Bucktown, Maryland. She had been abused repeatedly whilst a slave in Maryland and on one occasion, whilst she was attempting to protect one of her fellow slaves, she was hit over the head by an iron weight. This incident had occurred when Harriet was an early teenager, but she would continue to suffer from blackouts as a result of the head injury for the remainder of her life.

In 1849 she managed to escape from Maryland via the extensive Underground Railroad organisation set up by abolitionists and former slaves, finally reaching Philadelphia, Pennsylvania, where she succeeded in finding work as a maid. It was not long before Harriet had become involved in the very active abolitionist group in the city. In 1850 the Fugitive Slave Act made it illegal to help a runaway slave, and the following year Harriet embarked on her first mission with the Underground Railroad.

During the next ten years Harriet helped approximately three hundred slaves to escape, including her own parents, her sister and her sister's children. Her activities were always successful; she never lost a slave or became captured, despite the fact that there was a bounty out on her for $40,000.

During the Civil War Harriet worked as a nurse, scout and spy for the Union army in South Carolina. She was paramount in the freeing of some 750 slaves during the war, and for the destruction of large amounts of expensive Confederate property. She was given the nickname of 'Moses' by the slaves she had helped and inspired to start a new life in Canada, becoming the Underground Railroad's most famous leader.

After the war ended, Harriet returned to her home in Auburn, New York, where she had settled with her parents, expanding her work to include women's rights. By 1908 she had established a home for elderly and destitute black people, the Harriet Tubman Home. Harriet Tubman died in New York on 10 March 1913 at the assumed age of ninety-three.

CONFEDERATE
Van Dorn, Earl (1820–63)

Earl Van Dorn was born in Port Gibson, Mississippi, on 20 September 1820, and by all accounts, from an early age had a burning desire to become a soldier and to die gallantly and heroically. His appointment to West Point was obtained by the influence of his cousin, President Andrew Jackson, and Van Dorn graduated fifty-second of fifty-six in 1842, along with his classmates James Longstreet and William Rosecrans. In 1843 Van Dorn married Caroline Godbold from Alabama, who would bear him a son and a daughter.

He was posted to the infantry and was breveted first lieutenant for bravery at Chapultepec and during the battles in Mexico City. During the 1850s he served as a captain in the 2nd US Cavalry in Texas, and in 1858 was wounded three times during the fighting around Wichita Village in the Indian Territory, receiving promotion to major for his actions.

On 31 January 1861 Van Dorn resigned his commission in the US army and offered his services to the Confederate cause. It is reported that he said to his wife at the time:

Who knows, but that yet out of the storms of revolution, the dark clouds of war, I may not be able to catch a spark of lightning and shine through all time to come, a burning name. I feel greatness in my soul, and if I can make it take a shape and walk forth, it may be seen and felt.

He entered the Confederate army as a colonel, being ordered to travel to Texas, where his seizure of large amounts of US property, including three troop ships, was rewarded with promotion to brigadier-general. He was then sent to Virginia and promoted once more, to major-general (August 1861), where he led a division near Manassas.

He was then ordered by General Albert S. Johnston to join the Army of Tennessee, where he fought in the battle of Pea Ridge (March 1862), but his force was repulsed after two days of hard fighting, losing large numbers of men and being forced to retreat. His next instructions were to move east of the Mississippi, and having arrived too late to become involved in the battle of Shiloh (April 1862), he participated in the unsuccessful Confederate attempt to hold onto the Mississippi town of Corinth.

By June 1862, however, Van Dorn had left the Army of Tennessee and moved to Vicksburg under orders to defend the town. He managed to successfully repel a US naval attack here, and gave instruction to Major-General John C. Breckinridge to accompany the *Arkansas* to Baton Rouge (August 1862). The ensuing battle was a defeat for the Confederate command, but Van Dorn's actions had brought him to the attention of President Jefferson Davis, who ordered him to return to Mississippi to join General Price in the Army of the West.

His next mission was to attempt to retake Corinth (October 1862), the failure of which led to a court inquiry into Van Dorn's alleged negligent conduct during the battle. He was eventually acquitted of the charges against him, but many had become disenchanted with his efforts, and he was sent to the command of Lieutenant-General John C. Pemberton in charge of the cavalry troops, presumably under the supervision of the commanding officer. This proved, however, to be a more suitable placement for Van Dorn, who, in this role in early 1863, successfully raided Ulysses S. Grant's supply bases at Holly Springs, forcing the Union general to delay his schedule in the advance on Vicksburg. By March of the same year Van Dorn had another success at Thompson's Station, Middle Tennessee, whilst in command of a cavalry corps.

Van Dorn then moved his headquarters to Spring Hill, Tennessee, where he began a relationship with Jessie Helen McKissack Peters, the wife of a prominent local doctor. Van Dorn was reported to have been handsome, slim, elegant and something of a ladies' man, and Mrs Peters an incredibly beautiful woman. When Dr Peters returned from his year-long travels from home, he discovered the relationship and confronted Van Dorn on the issue. According to some accounts Peters threatened Van Dorn's life, and the general, begging for forgiveness, made a promise that he would write a public apology to the doctor if his life was spared.

Whatever the reason for, or circumstances of, this confrontation, Dr Peters shot Van Dorn in the back whilst he was sitting at a writing desk in his headquarters on 7 May 1863.

Van Dorn commanding Confederate troops at the battle of Corinth (October 1862). (Library of Congress)

Elizabeth Van Lew was born in Richmond, Virginia, on 12 October 1818 to one of Virginia's oldest and most prominent families. She studied in Philadelphia, and when she returned home had become outspoken about her anti-slavery views. When her father died, Elizabeth persuaded her mother to free their slaves, which she did.

When Virginia seceded and the battle of Fort Sumter forced the outbreak of war, Elizabeth appealed to Colonel Winder to be allowed to visit Union prisoners at the Confederate Libby Prison. Under the pretext of taking food and medicines, accompanied by her mother, to the Union prisoners, Elizabeth managed to acquire vital information from the prisoners about Confederate army movements, and thus embarked on her career as a Union spy.

Throughout the next four years Elizabeth not only continued to gather information from the prisoners, but also managed to extract information from the Confederate guards. She had set up a network of couriers and devised a secret code by which the prisoners would underline certain letters in the books she lent them.

At one stage she sent one of her servants into the home of Jefferson Davis to become a member of that household. She also sent her freed slaves, who had become family friends, on missions to Benjamin Butler and Ulysses S. Grant, who said to Elizabeth, 'You have sent me the most valuable information received from Richmond during the war.'

For her efforts during the war Grant made Elizabeth Postmaster of Richmond, a position she held for eight years from 1869 until 1877. Failing to be reappointed, and still receiving enormous criticism from the pro-Southerners in Richmond, she spent the rest of her life living on the annuity of the family of one of the Union soldiers she had befriended in Libby Prison. She died on 25 September 1900, and was buried in Shockoe Cemetery in Richmond. The people of Massachusetts had a gravestone erected in memory of her loyalty, which reads:

She risked everything that is dear to man – friends, fortune, comfort, health, life itself, all for the one absorbing desire of her heart – that slavery might be abolished and the Union preserved.

Elizabeth Van Lew's house in Richmond, Virginia. *(Library of Congress)*

Timothy Webster was born in Newhaven, Sussex, England, on 12 March 1822. At the age of eight he emigrated with his family to America, settling in Princeton, New Jersey, where in 1841 he met and married his wife, Charlotte Sprowles, with whom he had four children, two of whom died in infancy. Webster became a New York City policeman, and in 1854 was recommended to Allan Pinkerton as being suitable for detective work. He accepted the offer and became one of Pinkerton's most valuable detectives.

When war broke out Pinkerton was asked by George McClellan to enter the service of the Union army, and Webster joined him, becoming a Union spy. At Pinkerton's suggestion Webster moved his wife and children to Onarga, Illinois, close to Chicago, for their safety, and Webster posed as a Southerner in the Baltimore area.

Whilst Abraham Lincoln was travelling from Harrisburg to Washington for his inauguration ceremony (February 1861), Webster managed to uncover a plan by secessionists to assassinate the President-elect. He sent a message to Pinkerton, who managed to warn the presidential guards and save the life of the future President.

During 1862 Webster was exposed as a spy when he became too ill with rheumatism to report to Pinkerton. Two men called Lewis and Scully were sent by Pinkerton to locate Webster, but they were identified as spies and revealed information to the Confederate authorities about Webster. Despite the fact that Lewis and Scully were released, Webster was arrested, tried and sentenced to death by hanging.

The Confederate authorities ignored the threats of both Lincoln and Pinkerton that if Webster were to hang, then they would reciprocate by hanging the Confederate spies in their custody. After the first attempt to hang Webster was bungled when the noose slipped, he was hanged on 29 April 1862 and buried in Richmond.

In 1871, at the request of his widow and with the help of the Union spy Elizabeth Van Lew, Webster's body was located in Richmond and taken to Onarga, Illinois, where he was buried next to his son, Timothy Jr, who had been wounded at the battle of Brice's Crossroads and imprisoned in Mobile, Alabama, where he had died on 4 July 1864.

Timothy Webster's secret service head, Allan Pinkerton, in conference with Abraham Lincoln and General McClellan.
(National Archive)

William Wells was born in Waterbury, Vermont, on 14 December 1837. At the outbreak of the Civil War he enlisted as a private in the 1st Vermont Cavalry in September 1861, becoming a captain by November of the same year. After distinguished action at the battle of Orange Court House (August 1862), he was promoted to major, still commanding the 1st Vermont, on 30 December 1862.

By the summer of the following year Wells and the 1st Vermont were paramount in the repulse of J.E.B. Stuart's Confederate troops at Hanover, Pennsylvania (30 June 1863), and in the charge on Round Top in Gettysburg (July 1863). He had been imprisoned for two months from March until May, in Libby Prison, Richmond, but had been exchanged. Wells commanded the leading battalion in this cavalry charge under the command of General Farnsworth, who died during the attack. Within days, however, Wells himself had been wounded by a sabre cut at Boonsboro, Maryland.

Having recovered, he then became involved at the battle of Culpeper Court House (September 1863), where he was once again wounded and forced to recuperate. At the battle of Yellow Tavern, Virginia (11 May 1864), Wells commanded a battalion in Sheridan's Cavalry Corps, witnessing the death of J.E.B. Stuart. Sheridan was later to say of Wells, 'He was my ideal of a cavalry officer.'

Wells was again in command of a brigade in Custer's division at Tom's Brook, Virginia (9 October 1864), and at Cedar Creek (19 October), where his troops captured large numbers of artillery pieces. It was General Custer who informed Wells of the surrender at Appomattox, and he continued to command a division of the Army of the Potomac until it was reviewed in Washington on 25 May 1865.

Having served as adjutant-general of Vermont from 1866 until 1872, Wells was awarded the Congressional Medal of Honor for 'distinguished gallantry at the battle of Gettysburg, July 3 1863' in September 1891. He had been active in several veterans' associations until his death on 19 April 1892 in New York City. He is buried at Lakeview Cemetery, Burlington, Vermont.

Libby Prison in Richmond, Virginia where William Wells was held from March to May 1863. (National Archive)

(Library of Congress)

Joseph Wheeler was born on 10 September 1836 in Augusta, Georgia. He graduated from West Point in 1859 as a second lieutenant in the Regiment of Mounted Riflemen, briefly being posted to the Dragoons. He was assigned duty at Carlisle Cavalry School and then transferred to New Mexico, but in February of 1861 he resigned his commission and joined the Confederate army in Augusta the following month.

Leading an infantry regiment at the battles of Shiloh and Corinth, he was promoted to Chief of Cavalry in the Army of the Mississippi, leading them in the battles of Perryville (October 1862) and Murfreesboro (December 1862). During the Tullahoma Campaign Wheeler was given command of a corps, and leading them in the battle of Chickamauga (September 1863) he fought alongside Nathan Bedford Forrest. After conflicts between the two men and Braxton Bragg, Forrest was reassigned and Wheeler was placed in command of all the cavalry troops within the Army of Tennessee. In this role he led his men at Chattanooga (September–November 1863) and throughout the Atlanta Campaign, with responsibility for raiding the Union supply lines and attempting to hinder Sherman's march to the sea. He was unsuccessful in stopping Sherman, owing to the small force at his disposal.

Under the command of Wade Hampton in the Carolinas, Wheeler was captured in May 1865, after the Confederate surrender, and held at Fort Delaware for almost a month. During the Civil War he was in more than 500 skirmishes; commanded in 127 full-scale battles; had 18 horses shot from under him; and lost 36 staff officers from his side.

After spending some time in New Orleans after the war, Wheeler moved to Alabama in 1869, being elected its Congressman in 1880, but when volunteers were called for in the War with Spain he enlisted as a major-general of volunteers, seeing action once more in Santiago, Cuba and San Juan at the age of sixty-two. He retired with the rank of brigadier-general from the regular army in 1900, having earned the name 'Fightin' Joe' Wheeler. He died in Brooklyn, New York, on 25 January 1906, and was buried in Arlington Cemetery, being one of only a handful of Confederate soldiers to be buried there.

Index

Page numbers in *italics* refer to illustrations.